Ed Raduazo, photo

FOREWORD

Mud is a perfect material for art & building: easy, durable, beautiful. Unlike standardized industrial stuff, it varies a lot. Different earths do different things – or the same thing in a different way – but just about anything works, and if it doesn't, it lets you know so you can try something else.

I re-discovered mud about ten years ago, from a bunch of folks working with various natural materials: cob, adobe, strawbale, light clay, round wood, etc. They are teachers, activists, gardeners, writers, artists, or just folks wanting a better life. They taught me how to build a beautiful, practical, and cheap home out of mud. More importantly, they created a context in which art is a practical activity whose value is independent of galleries, interpretation, markets, money, and speculation.

To me, art means working for beauty before money. *Beauty,* as a medium for culture, craft, love, home, as well as a medium for exchange. Beauty as a vision of wholeness in a fragmented world. Beauty as an essential element of life, like air or water. Beauty as a way to nourish *living* culture. Beauty as a link to an unbroken chain of artists/craftsmen/humans whose hands have built homes and communities, grown food, delivered and taught children, and provided for the future. Beauty as a way of life, in which art is a common language — and participation is not a right to be won, but a simple and undeniable fact.

This (2d) edition only *begins* to show the range of earth-work by artist-builders all over. My part includes the best lessons I've learned as a result of saying "yes" (despite lack of experience & expertise) to labyrinths and sundials, unroofed mud sculpture and murals, and especially (inspired by the work of South African women), using pattern as a way to add life and beauty to industrial architecture. It all makes for a varied mix of possibilities. I hope you find something useful or interesting here.

More work may be printed in a new edition, or on a website (which needs a webmaster!) If you have community mud work you'd like to share, Hand Print Press invites you to send stories and pix to POB 576, Blodgett, OR, 97326, www.handprintpress.com.

Each contributor wrote their own description; I edited. Bios and photos (courtesy of each contributor) are on page 122. All other uncredited photos and illustrations, as well as errors, are mine.

— *Kiko Denzer, Oregon, April, 2005*

PS: For economy's sake, the "introduction" is at the back of the book, on page 114, so that most of these more expensive, full-color pages can be devoted to photos. For the same reason, and to give every project a bit of color exposure, the stories in the color section are "continued" on later pages, as in a magazine.

SECTION ONE

ART MADE WITH MUD, KIDS, & COMMUNITIES

WOODBURN HIGH

KIKO DENZER

Allie Luu, Jesús Vazquez, and the Woodburn High Art Club designed 14 sheetrock-backed panels to make their commons reflect more of the warmth of living that takes place below the high steel ceiling and cold, white walls. Art teacher Catherine Johnstone said response to the installation was not only positive, but "overwhelming." Panels this size need to be supported by rigid frames to prevent cracking, and to ease transport, storage, and installation. Better grade 2x4 lumber worked well for us on this project.

BEFORE

MUD MURALS: FIRST AID FOR AILING WALLS

KIKO DENZER

I got lost the first time I went to Fairplay School in Corvallis Oregon. In more than a hundred feet of red brick wall, there were five doors. Since the architecture didn't welcome visitors, someone had cleverly indicated the entrance with potted plants. I proposed to the students that we use an African-inspired mural to do what the architecture didn't: provide a welcome.

Inspiration came from Basotho women of Lesotho, South Africa, who annually decorate and protect their homes with beautiful earthen murals. Specific how-to is covered in section 2 (p. 33). For inspiration, see African Painted Houses, by Gary Van Wyk, (in Resources).

AFTER

MUD AT WALLS:

PER, GENINE COLEMAN

FAIRPLAY & CHAPMAN HILL SCHOOLS

KIKO DENZER

Earthen colors and simple geometry can humanize an uninviting space. Clearly, just human touch makes a surface more appealing, but perhaps more significant is how the geometric lines connect walls to doors to roof to ground. In both schools, we developed designs by drawing plants and patterns on paper; each student practiced their own design, in mud, on a piece of sheetrock before we made the mural.

For more on this particular style of pattern design, see pages 33 and following. For more about applied pattern and geometry in general, look up the works of Christopher Alexander, Soetsu Yanagi, and Jonathan Hale in the Resources section.

I also got lost at Chapman Hill School, in Salem. Staff had asked if we could do a tree sculpture (in mud in a carpeted library), I said I needed things from my car and took them outside. Walking back, I asked how many visitors got lost between the parking lot and the main entrance ('lots,' they said.) I showed them pictures from Fairplay to change their minds.

Before mudding, we wrapped the concrete column (at left) with re-cycled polypropylene baling twine so the mud had something to grab onto.

Additional text and photos start on page 76

"We started out by spreading the darker mud all over the wall. Then we used popsicle sticks to draw out the pictures. In certain spots we put light mud, like where the plants were. After that, we got a white, burnt rock [lime wash] to add details.... The pole was done in the same way."

— a student artist describes the process

A MANUAL FOR MAKING ART OUT OF EARTH   11

JEFFERSON SCHOOL
KIKO DENZER, OREGON

I declared that "we are all made of mud," and asked for drawings of the stuff of creation. A girl insisted we were made of bread and wine (she wasn't impressed when I told her that "Adam" was Hebrew for "red clay"). Others talked astrophysics and drew the big bang. Air was typically shown as spirals. Female faces represented the earth. I combined drawings into a composition. Younger artists (K-2) made impromptu bas-reliefs on a low section of brick wall (later hosed clean). The main mural has held for more than four years, uncoated, under a deep eave, with negligible wear. I hope another generation of artists will make a new one.

Jamie Topper, photos

KINZIE SCHOOL

JAMIE TOPPER, GENINE COLEMAN, CHICAGO

Deaf 4th and 5th graders depicted air, water, earth and fire. We bought powdered clay and sand in bags, as there was nowhere to dig nearby. Some kids didn't want to touch the mud and worried about their superfly sneakers. Some had never played with clay or sand! But slowly, then exuberantly, even the most uncomfortable kids smooshed clay through their fingers and delighted in texture and sculpting. We discussed where materials come from, how they came to be in bags. It was a little game, tracing things back to their origins in the earth. Fellow sculptor Genine Coleman and I worked with art teacher Marcia Florescu-Kauss and a sign interpreter. Gallery 37, a City arts education and job training program, sponsored us.

Rainer Warzecha, photos

UP FROM THE LARGE SCA

RAINER WARZECHA, MARK

Earth heads & Caves: from the inner vision of Rainer Warzecha, of Germany. "Children loved helping — as well as bathing in the mud-sea and sitting at an open fire. Then when we colored them — wow!" Built without foundations or roofs in 4-10 days.

A MANUAL FOR MAKING ART OUT OF EARTH   14

MUD: LE EARTHWORKS

LAKEMAN, KIKO DENZER, JAMIE TOPPER

*Earthen sundial by the author. A pole frame, covered with cardboard
and mud plaster; built by many volunteer hands in less than a week.*

A MUD VILLAGE IN GERMANY

RAINER WARZECHA, BERLIN

Oppposite: 'Earthhead-tower' 1999; Above: pavilion of global unity: 6 sculptures of children of all colors and races. Below: the kangaroo helps collect donations during the 6 week summer event — in winter it returns to a shelter in the sunny south.

Article & more pictures on pages 82-91

NEIGHBORHOOD MUD:
1ST AID FOR INTERSECTIONS

Starting in Portland, Oregon, neighbors in American cities are learning to transform plain old intersections into an American version of the European 'piazza' — but not with renaissance architecture and grand buildings. Rather, they begin by looking at what *isn't* there: a place for people to stop and talk to each other – a simple container for the basic ingredients of human culture – a place to sit, a smile, a handshake, a 'how do you do,' a cup of tea.

It started with a simple invitation.

Mark Lakeman decided to make a place for neighbors to meet, have a cup of tea, and visit. So he built a "T-hows" in

Continued on page 92

Sunnyside Piazza, SE 33rd & Yamhill, symbolizes the Sunnyside Neighborhood, and grew out of three months of potlucks and conversations between neighbors and was installed in a one day burst of creative expression. Jan Semenza and Lisa Weasel cordinated dozens of neighbors and business owners for blocks in all directions. Brian Borello assisted with laying out the Fibonacci spirals that anchor the design. (mL photo)

The Angel Bench, at SE 9th & Sherrett in Sellwood, recognizes the ancestral spirit of native peoples in the Portland area, imagined and expressed as one particular woman. A successful example of an all-weather exposed cob bench, it is finished with linseed oil and bee's wax. Janell Kapoor, Michael Bunch, and Lynne Dorian (pictured above) worked with dozens of people over ten days to create this place to linger and visit (May, 2003). (mL photo)

The City Repair Sauna, near SE 39th & Yamhill, was an ordinary garage. City Repair and other community members use it regularly and say "if you want to get naked with a bunch of hot and sweaty people, join City Repair!" Over several months in 2002, Amber Wiggett and Sukita Crimmell led over a hundred people in creating the sauna & gathering place.
(mL photo)

EARTH INSTALLATIONS
LABYRINTH & SUNDIAL, KIKO DENZER

Hundreds of volunteers collected materials, built, and hosted these installations for a summer festival. Thousands visited, learned, and occupied the "village" that grew up out of an empty field.

Continued on page 100

The labyrinth was surrounded by benches where people sat and watched, or ate wood-fired pizza from our earth oven. The design originates with the O'odham, "the people," or Pima and Papago, whose "Elder Brother" lived at the center of the earth, at the end of this path which he laid out to confuse his enemies.

The Greek Minotaur also lived in a labyrinth. A fourth century Algerian basilica holds a Christian version; the Kabbala contains a Jewish one; they are found in Hopi medicine wheels, Tibetan sand paintings, and ancient sites in Europe and the middle east. Unknown hands carved the first spiral labyrinth in rock, thousands of years ago. They may have been calendars; they're now often used for meditation (see Resources).

Ann Wiseman, photo

The shadow of the triangular gnomon ("know-mon") marks the hour on the bales around the edge. Inside is 100 cubic yards of sand – 10 dumptruck loads. So imagine those "sands of time" as representing 15 billion years since the Big Bang. By comparison, to represent the 10,000 year history of agriculture, would only require an oversize cup-full; to represent the 7 million years since our ancestors stood upright, would require a couple of 5 gallon buckets! Story-tellers used it as a stage for tales of how we began and where we've been. The whole thing was recycled after a week into firewood, compost, cattle feed, and an inch thick "top dressing" of sand for the field, which is swampy in winter.

SITE SPECIFIC SCULPTURE
SCHOOL SCULPTURES, KIKO DENZER

Kings Valley School, Oregon: About 40 young artists modeled ideas in clay and discussed them all before deciding (unanimously) to make this "dog cave" (the designer is the girl on the left). With more time and money, we would have had a stupendous playground. Everyone also made a small, cast concrete tile to set around the base. Cement stucco over mud sculpture solves some problems and creates others: concrete is waterproof, but it cracks, so more water gets in than out. The earth below can soften and move, and the cement shell can fail. But I've only had to do one repair on one sculpture in 6 years. Concrete is cheap, sustains rough use, and doesn't need a roof. It's also environmentally disastrous, caustic, and tricky.

Foster School, Sweet Home, Oregon: Students made clay models, voted on a class favorite. The sea monster was voted school favorite. We built it in a week.

Yaquina View School, Newport Oregon: Their mascot is a dolphin. Fisherman parents and some research revealed that hourglass dolphins, not the bottlenose variety common to TV, are the local variety. Two walkways linking parking lot to school made a perfect site. One mother complimented us on the work, but complained that "we can't get our kids away from that sculpture when we come to pick them up!" So the kids not only made art, they also transformed the space into a child-sized piazza, an outdoor gathering place and free space more inviting than the car!

A MANUAL FOR MAKING ART OUT OF EARTH   23

ENVIRONMENTAL PARK, MEXICO
KIKO DENZER

Alejandra Caballero and Paco Gomez invited me to help rural Mexican kids make several earthen ovens and sculpture for an environmental park/community center that included an organic garden, cooperative butchery, and health center. We began with a game of charades, acting out various indigenous animals (I'm the tail on the turkey above). Most popular were the spider (with legs of local juniper), turkey, squirrel and rabbit. Everyone made small models. The bigger pieces were built on "earthbag" cores (plastic feed sacks filled with earth and tamped into place). Earthen ovens are simple to build, and make the best pizza (see Build Your Own Earth Oven, in Resources).

Jamie Topper photo

TRIBUTE TO VOLUNTEER HANDS
JAMIE TOPPER, GENINE COLEMAN

I (Jamie) proposed a cob sculpture at Chicago's North Park Village Nature Center, a 40 acre urban preserve, to test the feasibility of natural building in our urban environment; both in terms of sourcing local materials and seeing how local cob holds up to our harsh winters. After two winters, there has been no cracking and no sign of serious degradation. A community based, site specific, large scale public art project, I think it has also been a successful introductory experiment in addresssing issues of sustainability. As far as I know, it is the only contemporary earthen structure in Chicagoland.

Continued on page 80

ALL HANDS KNOW HOW
LEARNING = BUILD

Ed Raduazo, photos

ABOVE: A STRUCTURE FOR PRE-SCHOOL CHILDREN, BY ED RADUAZO & FRIENDS:

"The youngest can walk in and out without ducking their heads; the oldest have to duck their heads a little — but there is no way an adult can go in or out gracefully.

"The rich red color is West Virginia clay from my friend Chris."

(Ed's wattle & daub birhouses are featured in a few more pages...)

ING = LEARNING

Building is innate. Combine kids, mud, leaves, sticks, pebbles, berries, twigs, and grass, soon you'll have homes, towns, and stories. Boys and girls are born builders, no less than birds and mud-daubing wasps.

The kids here were part of the Mexico project from page 24.

The model homes above were from the project on the next page (further described in the "notes" on page 115).

"Who knows but if men constructed their dwellings with their own hands, and provided food for themselves and families simply and honestly enough, the poetic faculty would be universally developed, as birds universally sing when they are so engaged?" — *Henry David Thoreau, Walden*

HOME IS...

DENZER & KLEINER

Once upon a time, a boy died at the hands of abusive adults who thought they were better because they had "bachelor's degrees," and "master's degrees." They thought they had the right to make decisions for others. Children were afraid of them – all but the boy who died; he believed that adults weren't better. He dared to say it, and refused to "cooperate." He paid the price for his courage. The rest of the kids secretly admired him, talked about him, remembered him, and even prayed to him. Eventually, they built a temple (model, above) to worship his memory. Their prayers and faith brought him back to earth as a god, and he created a free society where each person was respected and everyone lived in harmony.

The story (paraphrased) was written by a young man in a treatment center for "at-risk" youth who participated in a project described in the afterword. His (degreed) counselors required him to write a "more appropriate" story; the original disappeared into a confidential file. Later, he seemed relieved to have another story to read in public – an admission, perhaps, that he had been angry.

But the truth of the story remains. "Treatment" for the young man meant oppression: negotiating most of his waking acts with people who had power over him, and who evaluated and measured every action against institutional rules.

By contrast, we asked him and his peers to negotiate with each other and buckets of mud, to build model homes, write real stories about imaginary people

Continued on page 96

Above: A young man at work on his part of a village story project at the Corvallis (OR) Children's Farm Home, a treatment center for at-risk youth. Below: a village taking shape.

BUILDING
FOR
THE
BIRDS

ED
RADUAZO,
DISTRICT
OF
COLUMBIA

Ed Raduazo, photos, pp 30-31

BIRDHOUSE HOW-TO:

FRIENDLY, EASY, FUN

These houses were made for house wrens. They have a 4 inch diameter cavity, 6-8 inches deep, with a 1 inch diameter entrance, 1 to 6 inches above the floor. They must also be 6 to 10 feet above the ground in a bushy area or similar "edge habitat." Different birds have different requirements: door size (and height above floor), internal size, and height above the ground — not to mention habitat. The Complete Book of Birdhouse Construction for Woodworkers is cheap and has a fairly complete table; or try the library and/or internet.

MATERIALS & PREP:

1. *Scrap plywood, thin boards, etc. for a 5-1/2 inch circular base.*
2. *Thin sticks (around which to weave and apply mud plaster): I use split bamboo from my yard, but anything straight will do, about 1/4" thick.*
3. *Very thin, flexible twigs or vine for the horizontal wattle. Good wattle material includes willow, honeysuckle, grape vines, Karia Japonica, dogwood, etc. English Ivy is plentiful, non-native and invasive (hard to over-harvest). Two large trash bags supplies 14 builders.*

Continued on page 98

Mud works well on modern materials: The gate is mud-covered cardboard on wood; the mural behind is mud on sheetrock; "growth & form" (opposite) is a wall-hanging on sheetrock (in the catalog, Earth Art, by the author, Hand Print Press, 2004).

SECTION TWO

DESIGN AS
PROCESS
AND
PATTERN

DESIGN
AS A GROUP ACTIVITY

Art is a social activity. As Thoreau said, "It takes two to speak the truth. One to speak, and another to hear." Art made by a group needs a truth on which all agree, a framework in which to develop a workable design. A good theme is simple. Some of the ones pictured in this book include:

- "The elements of creation"
- a group identity, whether it's the school mascot (a dolphin) or a name ("The Fairplay Foresters")
- a favorite animal (acted out, drawn, or modeled and decided by vote)
- a place (in Mexico, kids made a mural of their hometown and called it "the most beautiful place in the world")
- a path for walking (labyrinths combine this with interesting history and sociology)

Or it can be a practical addition to landscape and/or architecture: benches, ovens, playground structures, bird houses, buildings, murals that add life to cold brick and concrete; even a solar clock, or sundial (which provides opportunities to explore technical and scientific topics, as well as history and sociology).

Participation is key: the more eyes at work, the more we see — and the more discussion, the more learning.

Look, imagine, tell stories, learn, argue and discuss, play charades, draw pictures, make models, discuss some more, take a vote!

I try not to make too many decisions before we start, because every project has different constraints, deadlines, budgets, participants, etc. That said, I do have some priorities for decision-making:

• Involve participants in as many decisions as possible, especially the early ones, like "What will we do?" "Where will we do it?" "Who gets to help?"
• Involve participants in as much of the work as possible: design, material and site prep, and cleanup.
• "Where there is no vision, the people perish." Discover or develop a strong vision. Look for good designs, drawings, and ideas. Articulate the vision; make sure the whole group "gets it." Drawings help, as do photos of other projects, written proposals, slide presentations, books, models, etc.
• Look for talent and gifts among all the participants; give them what they need in order to add to the project (I count participation, good will, and cooperation as gifts and talents equal to any other).
• Be positive; but not only about victories and success. Turn doubt and/or failure to advantage. For example: I didn't like an oven door that didn't work with the rest of a design. The architect I was working with said, "emphasize it. Give it it's proper value." Good advice. When I stopped focusing on my dislike, I could "make the most of it," which improved it in a way I could not have foreseen.

DESIGNING WITH PATTERN

I've tried two approaches to mural making: narrative, and pattern. Narrative takes a story or theme, illustrates it with characters, figures, landscape, and presents it, like a play. Famous examples include Michelangelo's bible stories on the Sistine Ceiling, Diego Rivera's depictions of Mexican history, and Picasso's outcry against the Spanish Civil War, "Guernica."

Narrative murals are great, but present challenges:

- they need a stage where the work can be seen, and an understanding audience;
- mural-makers need to agree on story, characters, and style;
- multiple elements make them complex to render visually;
- in order to succeed visually, each character or element of the story needs to be individually defined but stylistically related to every other element; but
- varying skill levels can create a visually conflicting hodge-podge of style, color, and quality.

There are additional challenges in any mural project:
- creating visual unity requires some degree of skill and experience;
- since a typical class will have many different skill levels, visual unity may require divisions of labor to integrate all the parts into a satisfying whole.

But pattern murals really only require basic drawing skills, and the ability to handle basic tools. With just a little time, almost anyone can become proficient, and the compositional challenges are more manageable. So I have found that pattern murals offer an excellent way to meet most mural challenges. In addition, if your goal is unity, there are other benefits, both visual and social:
- simple pattern exercises can be used with *any* age group to produce very sophisticated results, not only in mural design, but also in such valuable lessons as visual analysis, proportion, drafting, enlargement, and composition;
- unlike figure or narrative drawing, the visual appeal of a pattern doesn't depend quite so much on skill, so it's rare that anyone's work looks "out of place."
- because patterns are simple and repetitive, it is easier to discuss and decide which patterns to use and how to combine them in a good composition;
- because the process is simple, participants can identify their part in it, even if their design wasn't "chosen," or they didn't "get to put mud on the wall."
- **visually, pattern murals are usually a stronger and more positive addition to a building than narrative murals.**
I think this last benefit is worth talking about a bit more:
The geometric structure of a pattern mural creates a series of powerful visual centers that unify, clarify, and *give real*

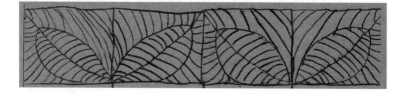

life to concepts like "entrance," "pathway," and "public space."

This is rare in industrial architecture, and for good reason: modern materials come in identical, machine made units. Most often, they are engineered to be installed with machines, at high speed, and with minimal human involvement. Visually then, designs tend to be defined by those "units:" pieces of sheetrock that are 4 x 8 feet (or larger); concrete that is often cast a whole wall at a time; and/or perfectly identical blocks or bricks that are sometimes even pre-set in huge panels and hung from a steel frame.

Typically, in buildings made this way, there is little visual detail, and so your eye sees just one *immense* shape that may be many, *many* times larger than you. The closer you get, the larger it looms. Without surface detail on a human scale, your eye and brain can't relate to the building. As a result, you may also find yourself confused (as I was at Fairplay School, unable to distinguish between the entrance door and the (locked) boiler room door, p. 8). Or you may feel lonely and small (as the kids at Woodburn High felt in their high-ceilinged commons, p. 6). This is not "just" an emotional response, but a fact of nature. Indeed, science and psychology recognize that "sensory deprivation" can cause serious physical and psychological damage.

In all sculptural projects I've worked on, however, and *especially* in the pattern-mural projects, I have had very clear responses that the work is not superficial *decoration,* but an effective *re-building* or *renewal* of a part of the environment (especially at entrances, which shape our first impressions).

This is a practical application of beauty that doesn't often get discussed. If you're interested, however, many related ideas and examples can be found, especially in the writings of architect Christopher Alexander. Look for *A Pattern Language,* and more recently, *The Nature of Order.* Both books are expensive, but if your library doesn't have them, ask if they can order them; see Resources for details on these and other titles.

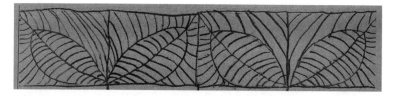

FINDING PATTERN

INSPIRATION IS EVERYWHERE; draw it from life around you: go outside, look at real plants, landscapes, animals, or at least draw from photos.

- Which are the biggest shapes, patches of light and/or dark, shapes within shapes?
- Choose the biggest, and surround it/them with an imaginary frame (or try cutting a square, paper-shaped hole out of the center of a piece of paper. Look through it to "frame" what you want to draw).
- Use your *whole* sheet of paper for your frame. Draw the biggest shapes/light or dark areas, etc. Your lines should go from one edge of your paper to the other.
- Simplify what you see — no exact copies required.
- Fill in darker areas to reveal patterns.
- *Don't erase,* but *do* study your work; identify the best lines.
- Make as many drawings as you need to get one you like.

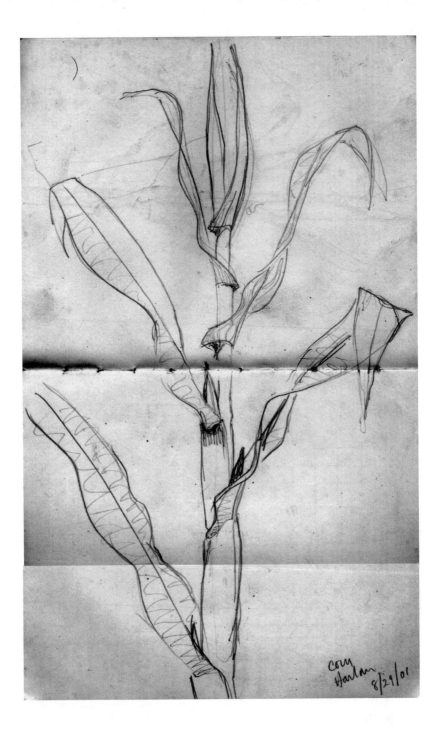

cory
Harlan
8/29/01

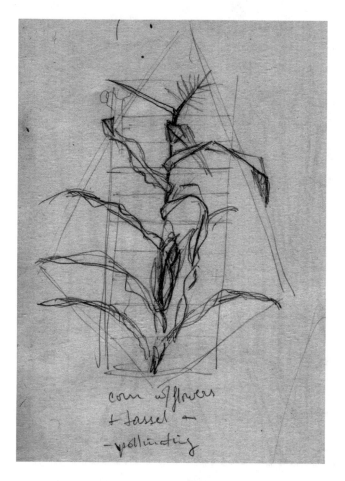

corn w/flowers
+ tassel —
— pollinating

FINDING INSPIRATION

These pages (from my sketchbook) are how I developed a wall pattern at "Intaba's Kitchen," a restaurant in Corvallis, Oregon. Every design has its challenges and lessons, so it helps to keep a sketch & notebook! I was growing corn at the time. Like other plants, corn grows according to a pattern. Drawing helped me answer these questions:

- What's the biggest shape? (Note the diamond frame.)
- What elements repeat? (Note horiz. lines at each leaf.)
- What elements change? (Each leaf shorter than last.)
- Where are the centers? (Meeting of vertical and horiz.)
- What patterns can you see?

FITTING GEOMETRY TO SPACE, 1

Sketching and thinking on paper transformed the triangular design (based on the original corn drawing) into a rectangular pattern with strong diagonal elements. Patterns change depending on your point of view. I started to focus more on the layering of individual leaves, a pattern that is also strong in the allium (onion) family.

The rectangle determined proportion. In the drawing on page 43, I found that two sets of three lines made a stronger (more triangular) pattern than sets of 4 lines.

Any drawing, any shape, has proportion, which is the relationship of one element to another (length to width, width to height). Proportion is key to geometry, geometry is key to pattern, pattern is always proportional.

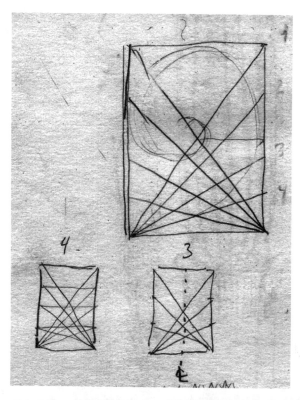

DONE!

Below is a section of the finished wall showing the pattern as sculpted in relief. I used metal trowels to apply an earthen plaster to a cob wall.

The making of the restaurant was a community event coordinated by owner Ocean Liff-Anderson. Many community members learned about earth as a building material by jumping into the mud (more about that story at intabas.com).

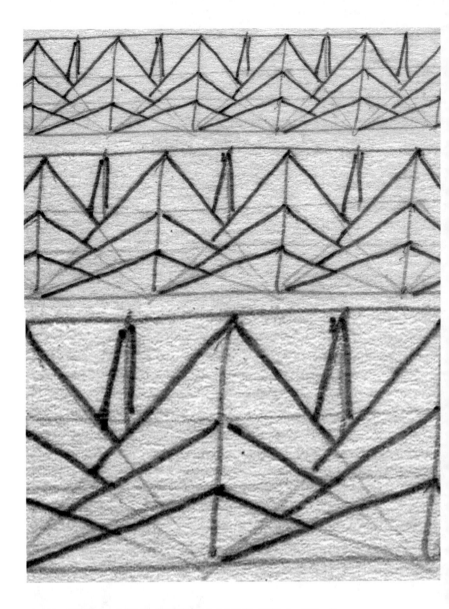

FITTING GEOMETRY TO SPACE, 2

The progression from large to small as the pattern rises is natural — like a tree trunk dividing into branches, twigs, and leaves; plant stems that divide and get thinner as they rise; or the familiar illusion by which a wide road narrows as it recedes into the distance.

The greater density of detail at the top helped break up the mass of the wall, making it appear lighter as it rises (see photo of the actual wall on previous page).

Getting the design onto the wall involved laying out a grid and finding a rhythm for sculpting many copies of the same pattern.

FITTING GEOMETRY TO SPACE, 3

There is far more to the geometry of architecture than I know, and certainly more than I can cover here (see Resources), but I've been learning about it by making roughly measured drawings of a building, applying the simplest geometry, and seeing where it takes me.

The example here is from the Fairplay School Mural. I used the measured drawing to produce a small-scale, blank plan that I could duplicate and use for testing different designs, patterns, and color schemes.

Since each student drew one, I had hundreds of patterns to choose from (see the pattern excercise that follows this section) — but three jumped out at me as being best for the wall. I don't remember even trying any of the others, though many were beautiful.

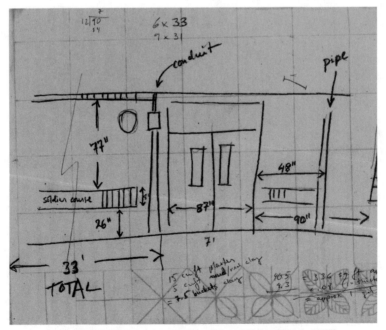

MEASURED PLAN DRAWING OF MURAL SITE

PATTERN DRAWINGS

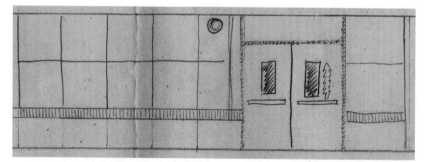

SKETCH OF MURAL SITE, TO SCALE, & DIVIDED BY GRID

SCALE SKETCH WITH PATTERN DRAWINGS ADDED

A MANUAL FOR MAKING ART OUT OF EARTH

MIRROR IMAGES MAKE PATTERNS THAT MOVE

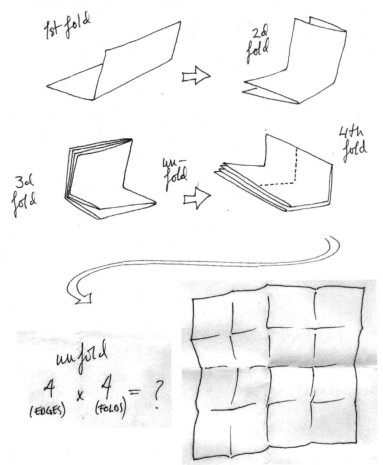

1st fold

2d fold

3d fold

un-fold

4th fold

unfold

$$4 \text{ (EDGES)} \times 4 \text{ (FOLDS)} = ?$$

START WITH A PIECE OF PAPER
1. FOLD IN HALF,
2. AND HALF AGAIN
3. ONCE MORE; THEN OPEN & FOLD THE OTHER WAY
4. FOUR FOLDS, UNFOLDED, MAKES HOW MANY SECTIONS? (HINT: WHAT'S FOUR TIMES FOUR?)

DRAW YOUR PATTERN IN ONE CORNER. PRESS *HARD!*

FOLD

THEN *RUB* THE BACK OF THE PAPER WITH THE OTHER END OF THE PENCIL, OR ANYTHING SMOOTH. PRESS *HARD!*

TRACE OVER THE LINES TO MAKE THEM ALL DARK

RE-FOLD AND REPEAT TO DOUBLE YOUR PATTERN

$2 \times 2 = 4!$

$4 \times 4 = 16!$

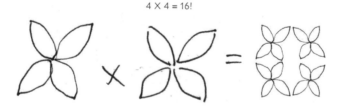

DRAW, FOLD, RUB, REPEAT
1. USE A SOFT BLACK ART PENCIL (4B TO 6B)
2. DRAW INSIDE ONE RECTANGLE; PRESS HARD
3. FOLD,
4. RUB THE BACK OF THE PAPER, HARD!
5. UNFOLD,
6. TRACE OVER THE LINES THAT RUBBED OFF,
7. AND REPEAT...

ONE:
**THE
ORIGINAL
DRAWING**

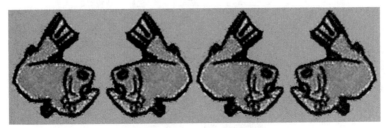

TWO:
**SIMPLIFIED, THEN REVERSED &
REPEATED, MAKES RHYTHM**

THREE:
**FURTHER SIMPLIFIED TO MAKE A DESIGN
ANYONE CAN DRAW IN MUD (AS ABOVE)**

DRAW, REPEAT, & REVERSE
FOR RHYTHM & DESIGN!

1. Repeat a drawing, Repeating lines should simplify, strengthen, and unify the pattern.
2. Reverse each repetition, drawing as from a mirror: the pattern will develop a rhythm and create a whole new design (if free-hand is too hard, use the soft-pencil technique on the previous page).
3. Of the patterns below, one fills more of the paper. Which is stronger? Why?
4. One pattern is built on a diagonal and the other is built on a cross. Which one has more rhythm? Why?

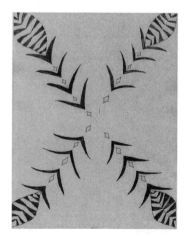

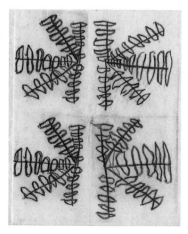

SECTION THREE

MUD
RECIPES

Earthen plaster on sheetrock: "leaf/life" & "schooling salmon," from the catalog, Earth Art, by the author, Hand Print Press, 2004.

"COB," "SUPER COB," PLASTERS, AND OTHER MUD

A BRIEF INTRO TO VARIETIES OF MUD

Most cultures use earth for building; it is the most common construction material on the planet. For comfort, beauty, ease of use, ecology and economy, it beats most other materials hands down. If you're already familiar with earthen building, you may not learn anything new here. If you're new to mud, you'll learn more from doing than from reading, so get started quickly, then read more as needed.

"Cob" is a traditional British name for a convenient, durable structural building material that typically contains a mix of clay-soil, sand, grit, gravel and/or small stones, and straw. "Adobe" is a similar mixture, more of this and less of that, but made into bricks that are dried, and laid up in mud-mortar. (The word comes from arabic, "al-toba" meaning "the brick.")

Earthen building traditions adapt their material in a variety of ways to create fine decorative and/or sculptural detail. This finer material is typically called "plaster," a generic term that is and has been used to mean everything from real, under-your-feet mud, to gypsum plaster, to stucco (either the old-fashioned kind made of lime and sand, or the post WWII kind made with Portland cement, sand, and lime), to traditional African mixes of manure and clay. Any mud can be "plaster," and most plasterers call their material "mud."

Numerous books, new and old (some are in the resource section), will tell you all about working with mud. All I want to do in this small book, however, is give you enough info to get started and get excited. As soon as you get dirty, you'll learn, and the questions you can't answer by your own trial and error will surely lead you to find the info you need.

GETTING MUDDY; FINDING CLAY-SOIL

Soil comes in layers: topsoil is a mix of organic matter (decomposed plants) and inorganic matter (rock, sand, silt, clay). Especially when it's full of worms, compost, humus, and lots of organic matter, topsoil is best for your garden. Below, however, is subsoil, which may contain anything from pure sand and rock to pure clay that you could use to make pottery.

What you're looking for is subsoil containing *some* clay — just enough to make it sticky when wet and, when dry, hard and strong. Dry, it should feel solid, fairly dense, and tough — a bit like concrete. Indeed, cob or adobe *was* the first concrete! (For more about dirt, clay, and where they come from, look up a wonderful book called *Dirt, the Ecstatic Skin of the Earth,* in the resource section.)

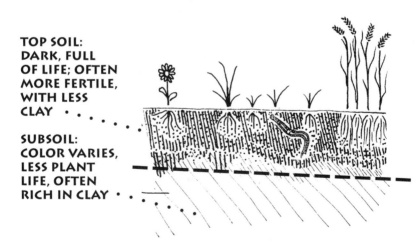

TOP SOIL: DARK, FULL OF LIFE; OFTEN MORE FERTILE, WITH LESS CLAY

SUBSOIL: COLOR VARIES, LESS PLANT LIFE, OFTEN RICH IN CLAY

RECOGNIZING CLAY

Clay in your subsoil has distinct and recognizable characteristics. It's harder to dig, and doesn't crumble easily. A shovel leaves a shiny cut mark. When dry, it will be hard and not crumbly. When wet, it grabs boots and tires and won't let go. Dry or wet, however, it will feel slippery and "greasy;" because clay particles are flat, and slide across one another smoothly, instead of rolling and grinding.

Having said all that, it's not hard to mistake fine silt for clay. Often, however, even silt can be sticky enough to use. The best thing to do is try some, and see how it works. As an old English cobber said, "I never met a subsoil I didn't like."

If you can't find clay-soil or anything workable on your site, look for old quarries, riverbanks, ponds, road cuts, building sites, and neighbors' yards. Be careful too. Fill dirt from developed sites or old dumps may be full of broken glass or dangerous debris, and depending on where you dig, you may need to ask permission. And if you absolutely can't find clay soil, you can often find "waste" clay from a local potter, or from a ceramics shop at the local high school or college. In a real pinch, you

can buy pure "fireclay," dry and powdered, from a building supplier; around here, it costs less than $10 for a 40 or 50 pound bag.

drawing by Ann Sayre Wiseman

A QUICK AND DIRTY "SNAKE" TEST

Take a pinch of dirt in your palm, spit into it, and mix it with a finger. Silt or organic matter feels floury or crumbly. Clay feels sticky, slippery, and a bit greasy. Take a bit more and add enough water until you can roll it into a snake. See how long a snake you can make. If you can get a couple of inches or more, roll your hand over flat. Will your snake bend without breaking? The longer snake you can make, and the easier it bends without breaking, the more clay you have. At minimum, you should be able to roll and bend at least two inches of a 3/8" thick snake.

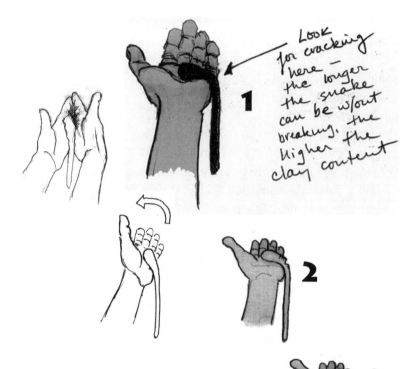

Look for cracking here — the longer the snake can be w/out breaking, the higher the clay content

THE FIRST SNAKE IS SOIL RICH IN CLAY; THE SECOND IS PROBABLY JUST FINE, TOO; THE THIRD ONE, WELL, LET'S MAKE A TEST BATCH AND SEE HOW IT WORKS....

A SLOW AND NERDY "SHAKE" TEST

This test uses water, agitation, and time to separate soil into large, small, and smallest. While NOT necessary for identifying good building material, it does make a good science experiment which can be well adapted for students at every grade level (indeed, the shake test is a standard tool for engineers and soil scientists).

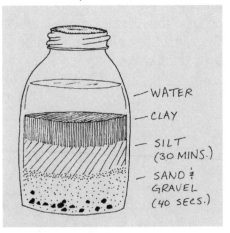

As in a lake or river, sand and gravel settle out first, then silt, then clay. The trick is timing. You can't tell by just looking which is clay. Use a watch.

So: pulverize some soil to dust; if it's wet, mash it like potatoes. No lumps! If not not pulverized, clay lumps sink like stones and you may be fooled into throwing away perfectly good material.

Fill a clear glass jar, half to two-thirds soil, and the rest water; you can add a teaspoon of salt or liquid soap to help the clay settle faster. Shake hard 'til thoroughly homogenous.

Now look at your watch: if everything settles solid and the water clears in less than 1/2 hour, you'll know for sure that you don't have any clay! Ideally, you'll have some rocks and sand (they'll settle out in less than a minute); then you'll have some silt (that settles out in about 30 minutes); then what's left in solution after 30 minutes is clay.

So at 30 minutes, I make a mark at the point between what has settled and what is still in solution. Sometimes it can be hard to tell, but generally, what's in solution will sloosh around a bit, while anything that has truly settled won't move, even when you tilt your jar from side to side.

There's a large range of workability: some soils settle in

just over a half hour with a large amount of very silty clay. Others contain mostly grit and fine sand and a very thin layer of very fine clay — just enough to hold everything together. Some are pure clay that you can use to make pottery.

PREPARING YOUR WORK SPACE

Even with mud, organized space for tools, materials, etc., all makes it easier. If you expect rain, prepare accordingly.

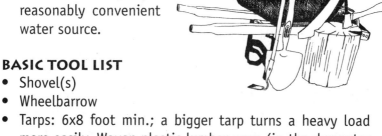

- Decide where to store materials (piles of sand and dirt),
- Locate a hose or other reasonably convenient water source.

BASIC TOOL LIST

- Shovel(s)
- Wheelbarrow
- Tarps: 6x8 foot min.; a bigger tarp turns a heavy load more easily. Woven plastic lumber wrap (in the dumpster at the lumber yard) is strong, free, recyclable "waste." Tyvek or Typar housewrap also works, and scraps are sometimes available at construction sites.
- Containers of various sizes (5-gallon plastic pails are most useful, followed by 1 and 2 gallon sizes, and quart and 1/2 gallon yogurt pots — all of which you should be able to find for free or close to it. The larger ones are commonly thrown away by large commercial kitchens, contractors, etc. The smaller ones show up at recycle centers.)
- Electric drill with a metal paint-mixing attachment (should be a 1/2" drill, or heavy-duty 3/8" model).
- Plaster tools (trowels, knives, forks, spoons, spatulas, brushes of all sizes, bits of plastic pipe and tubing, etc.), as well as scrap lumber of various lengths and sizes.
- Old clothes to get dirty in, and boots if you don't want to go barefoot.

MORE TOOLS

- Hardware cloth (1/4 or 1/2 inch), on a 2x2 foot or larger wood frame; for screening sand, soil, and straw; expanded metal lath or any other heavy mesh works, especially if stiff enough to need no frame. Beware sharp edges that grab unsuspecting flesh!
- Machete, hatchet, or weed whacker and large garbage can.
- Spray bottle/mister.

BASIC MUD RECIPE

1. One part clayey, sticky soil (this is the binder that holds it together). I try to work with what's underfoot. And of course, barefoot is best, but if you think there's any chance of finding glass or nails in your soil, or just sharp stones — then boots are good.
2. 1-4 parts coarse or "sharp" sand (beach sand is too round).
3. Water.
4. Straw (for flexible strength, like re-bar in concrete).

For structural or "super cob," it's important that the straw be long and tough so that it holds everything together even when wet. For plasters, it's important that fibers be short, uniform, and fine, so that you can get a nice smooth finish and sharp details. Make test bricks before you build. Remember, too much sand makes it weak. Too much clay makes it shrink and crack.

In 3 days, three of us mixed "super cob" and roughed out this 25-foot long wall to full height. The arch was made with straps of straw and mud (no sand) tied onto a bamboo framework fixed in the wall.

BIG MUD FOR STRUCTURAL USE: "SUPER COB"

What makes "super cob" super is the ease and speed made possible by mixing *very* wet, and using the longest straw you can find. The long fiber holds the wet mud in place without "splooging," even up to heights of 2 or more feet. ("Long," in this case, means at least 12-16 inches, but bales vary, so check before you buy.)

I make a donut of sand on my tarp, put the clay-soil in the middle, add water, and dance until the mud is smooth and yogurty. Then I pull in sand, adding water to keep it yogurty. Then I spread it out thin – a couple of inches or so, sprinkle with straw, and tramp around, *without folding or mixing,* until the straw is all muddy. If a bit of yogurt squishes up, I add straw. Then I pull the ends of the tarp to roll the mud into a big burrito, and step on it with my full weight. It sinks (or "splooges") just a couple of inches. I've also made super cob by mixing about half a yard in a pit. When I can't add any more straw, it's done! Total straw: maybe a 3" flake per 15 gallons of sand, or nearly a 3-string bale per yard?

I apply hand- or fork-fuls, and wiggle or stomp it into place, keeping the edges as square and vertical as possible as it goes up. Sticks fixed in the mud can serve as armatures on which I might tie loaves or "straps" of super cob. Or if weight is an issue, I'll take a thin layer of pure straw and spread it with gooey mud (pure clay-soil and water mixed to peanut butter consistency). Rolled and kneaded into loaves, it can be wrapped around armatures, tied in place, and/or molded into free-standing structures that will dry strong and relatively light. (They can also take a long time to dry.)

All the straw will make your cob look like a furry beast. Detail can be impossible, so I'll build up a mass of mud to carve away – which you can do quite wet – or let it dry (more or less), and carve it like soft stone, with a machete or hand-axe.

You'll need a foundation if you want your work to last. If you get ambitious and want to make big, permanent sculptures, read up a bit on foundations (see Resources).

Kids at the Foster School in Sweet Home, Oregon, mixing mud on a tarp. To turn the material, stand in the middle of the tarp, grab an edge, and pull the tarp towards you, while walking backwards. Don't roll your mud onto the ground! Lay tarp out flat. Stomp and turn, stomp and turn.

MUD FOR WALLS: PLASTER BASICS

Plaster is typically a sandier mix that sticks well to most surfaces. Textured walls help it stick, but texture isn't always necessary (depending on thickness — the thicker and heavier the layer, the more texture you'll need). A thin plaster sticks beautifully to plain old sheetrock. I have applied it successfully to masonry, masonite, and even glass! Very fine mud may work better on a smooth surface.

Mud sticks to wood, too, but since wood swells and shrinks, it must be covered with a layer of tarpaper or other waterproof barrier, followed by textured material for the mud to "grab." Otherwise, it cracks and falls off when the wood moves. Expanded metal lath, is typical for cement stucco, but "grab" material can be improvised. Baling twine (stapled or nailed down every few inches) is cheap or free, and won't rust. Whatever you use, however, it should be well attached so the weight of the mud won't pull it off (and nails should be galvanized).

A PLASTER RECIPE

1. One part clay soil.
2. Three to four parts sharp mason's sand or concrete sand (finer sand means better detail – but not beach sand!)
3. Just enough water (test it; too much causes slumping/cracking).
4. One half part (more or less) fine fiber (short stuff (1/2" or less) is best for detail work and thin mural plasters).
5. Optional: a dollop of wheat paste or other binder.

About fiber: Use what's easily available; options include:

- **Manure** (horses, cows, etc.) It's important that they be eating grass (vs grain). I prefer cow to horse manure as it's uniformly shorter and finer. Manure also makes more weather-resistant plaster. I've not tried sheep, goat, rabbit, or deer manure, but imagine they'd work as long as the animals were eating grassy fiber. Use gloves as needed.
- **Chopped straw:** easiest to sweep the floor of a barn, but a machete works – be careful! Or use a string-type weed-whacker in a big garbage can (do it on a tarp to catch the bits), or a leaf shredder.
- **Cattail** or other seed bearing fibrous fluff: try to harvest when it's loose and comes off the stem easily; you may also find it easier to mix it with your water *before* you add the water to the mud.
- **Miscellany:** I've tried many things, from newspaper (short, weak, not very good), to horsehair (great! but you need the shorter body hair), to finely chopped bits of sisal twine. Maybe dryer lint? Try it and see!

Combine sand and clay. Mixing on a tarp is fun, but you can use a wheelbarrow – or a cement mixer, in a pinch.

A tarp makes room for group fun. Pour the sand in a circle in the center of the tarp, so it's like a donut. Dump the clay-soil in the center, add water, and mash until smooth and sticky. If you're using wetted fiber (manure or paper pulp), add it right to the clay-soil.

Use the tarp to "fold" the sand into the mud by lifting

the edge of the tarp and pulling back (you stand in the center of the tarp and pull while walking backwards). Mix it a bit dry at first, until the clay-soil and sand are well mixed.

Then add water and dance. I usually make my plaster no stiffer than peanut butter, often wetter, depending on the application. It's easier to start dry and add water as you need it, sometimes just by putting a dribble of water in your bucket and mixing a few handfuls at a time as you put it on the wall.

If you're using dry fiber, liked chopped straw, add it last, fold, stomp, and add more water as needed.

Additional binders: Wheat paste and other binders can make your plaster both stickier and smoother. I add it as needed. To a wheelbarrow-full of plaster, I might add a cup or two of paste (less if I'm using dry powder). I go by feel more than exact measure – I stop when the mud goes from feeling sandy and loose to "fatty" and cohesive.

Make wheat paste out of a thin batter of flour and cold water (no lumps!); cook it on low, or add it to boiling water, and stir 'til you have thick glue. (You can also buy it in dry powdered form at the paint store — but beware the new synthetic vinyl stuff.) You can also use common white glue (made of casein, or milk protein — thus the cow on the Elmer's glue label). Yellow carpenter's glue is fine, if more expensive. Glue may make your mud more "water-resistant," but also less breatheable, hard to recycle, and more expensive.

PUTTING MUD ON THE WALL: "HARLING," & OTHER TRICKS TO MAKE IT STICK

Use trowels or just schmear it on by hand. Thickness can vary from a quarter inch to an inch or two or more. Thicker is trickier, as heavy mud may sag, crack, or fall off – unless you give it more texture to "grab" onto. When you've covered as much wall as you can comfortably work on, smooth the surface with circular strokes. Use trowels, a block of wood, or hands. Trowels and wood-blocks make a flat, smooth surface; hands make beautiful textures, everything from deep finger and hand-prints, to subtly undulating surfaces that catch the light to make beautiful shadow-play. Experiment! It's guaranteed to produce expertise.

In the old days, when people protected their homes with traditional lime-sand stucco, they would engage in an activity called "harling" (perhaps a variant of "hurling"?)

To harl mud, take a small handful and "splot" it onto the wall. Your hand should be about 12-16 inches away. You may have to adjust distance and force according to the mud, wall, and your arm. Roll or jiggle each handful a bit so it coheres — otherwise, the mud may splatter instead of sticking to the wall in a nice round "dot." Sometimes adding a bit of wallpaper paste is just the thing.

The dots should be spaced closer for a thick layer, farther apart for a thin layer.

I work in sections, sized according to how fast the mud is drying and how quick I'm working. Once a piece of wall is nicely dotted, I use a trowel to smooth one into the next — always working a fresh dot into an already troweled section. Some dots fall off, but in general, you should find that you can cover a lot of surface FAST!

IF YOUR MUD WON'T STICK

1. Wet the wall with water. Spray it with a hose or a spray bottle, or use a big brush to paint it on. You'll need to follow with mud quickly, before it dries.
2. If the water doesn't work, try pure clay-soil, thinned with water until it's like thick paint. This also gives you a bit more working time, since it dries slower, and often adds enough "stickum" that it will hold the plaster even after it dries.
3. For a stickier alternative, make a paint with wallpaper paste and mud, and maybe a bit of sand or coarse chopped straw for extra texture. Add water as needed.

MUD-DRAWING TRICKS

- On your wall, measure out a grid similar to the paper grid of the pattern exercise. Plaster one section at a time, draw the design while the mud is nice and soft, and move on.

- A grid makes enlarging your design easy, and teaches proportion: divide paper design and mud "canvas" into halves, quarters, etc.; copy the design section by section.

A FINE COLLECTION OF EXPENSIVE, HARD-TO-FIND SCULPTING TOOLS...

- Different mud, tools, & technique all produce different qualities of line. Fingers work different than fingernails, smooth plastic is different than wood, metal than plastic, etc.

- A tool held perpendicular to the mud will make a ragged line, but at a low angle, it will make a clean line.

- Texture adds vitality and depth (especially when colored), and increases visual impact. Experiment! Fingers make nice texture, as do brushes, combs, shells, sticks, thin lines, thick lines, fork tines, maybe twine, or even fish spines! OK, blame the rhymes for the spines, but seriously, anything can be a tool — try it!

COLOR

I collect natural earthen pigments when I see them in road cuts or construction sites. Various shades of yellow, orange, red, brown, and black are all common around my home in the central coastal region of Oregon and in the Willamette Valley. Less common, but not that unusual, are white, (greyish) blues, greens, and even purple! However, if you don't have easy-to-

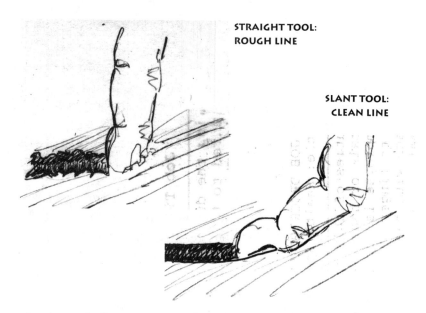

STRAIGHT TOOL:
ROUGH LINE

SLANT TOOL:
CLEAN LINE

get color underfoot, concrete pigments work well (Davis colors, for example). Many are various forms of iron oxides, quite potent in small amounts, and relatively cheap at the builder's supply.

If you want more colors and decide to explore other sources of pigments, use *extreme* caution. Some pigments, especially some of the blues and greens used by potters for glazing, can be highly toxic in their raw form; some contain toxic heavy metals. And any powder can be hazardous to the lungs. Avoid breathing the dust.

Colors can be mixed into the plaster itself or applied on the surface of the finished plaster. Mixed with water, or a binder (wallpaper paste, waterglass, casein (milk protein), etc.) you get home-made paint (see *Natural Plasters* & *Hand Sculpted House,* in Resources). Or try the ancient cave technique of blowing dry powder onto the wall itself.

The Fairplay and Chapman Hill murals were "fixed" with a 50:50 waterglass:water solution to make them harder and water-resistant. Then I mixed pigments with waterglass and applied the color to the surface. See the next section for more on waterglass.

(RE)CREATION IS THE BEST PRESERVATION

The best way to "preserve" art is to create it, and re-create it, again and again. The Basotho culture of South Africa is a good example, where the women practice their tradition by making new murals every year (*tradition* comes from Latin, and means "to hand over.")

How long will earthen art last? Maybe as long as the hills. Untreated mud *is* durable, especially in protected places away from severe winds and the heaviest rain.

At times, however, I've used a binder to protect earthen art against water, abrasion, and abuse, or sometimes just to carry pigments in ways that are visually appealing.

People ask about adding cement, but Portland cement and mud make a bad mix. Cement is caustic, so it makes the mud caustic; it is also non-recycleable, non-breatheable, and attracts moisture like a sponge, so it's wet and cold to the touch – unlike mud, which feels warm and dry. By the same token, mud makes concrete weaker and softer. (But they can work beautifully together if you don't actually combine them – see the next section on "casting stories in stone.")

"WATERGLASS" FOR PROTECTION & PAINT

Waterglass has become my preferred binder in places where it's needed. The chemical name is sodium or potassium silicate. It's an inert mineral compound similar to window glass, but under heat and pressure, it's soluble in water. I get it from a ceramic supplier for $9 a gallon. It's clear, viscous, and pours like heavy cream. It dries into a clear, brittle substance that crushes to a fine powder, but it has significant binding power, and is used in some refractory cements, as well as numerous other industrial applications.

I've only discovered it in the past few years, so I'm still learning, but it has made murals possible in less protected areas where I might not have risked it before. It does interesting things with color. And it's cheap!

Mixed 50:50 with water and sprayed (or brushed) onto

dry mud and allowed to dry again slowly, waterglass will bind the mud to a significant depth, preventing damage from rain, hoses, and curious fingers (but not hostile ones). Brushed on, it soaks in deeper, binds more, and may darken colors.

Mixed with pigment, it produces wonderfully varied mottling: more opaque in deep areas, where the pigment settles thicker, and more transparent on raised surfaces.

A 50:50 mix will treat approximately 30 sq ft per gallon — more if you spray, less if you use a brush and really saturate the mud. More saturation provides more strength and water-resistance. If you want to stretch your supplies a bit more, you can dilute it with a little more water.

Make sure to really fill every nook and cranny, otherwise, you end up with uncemented areas which will be fragile. When applying it, especially over deeply textured mud, it's almost as if you're pouring it on with the brush. As you'll see, it soaks in so fast you don't really have time to brush it. Strange stuff.

Spray bottles are a good way to apply it, especially if you want a thinner application. Coarse rather than fine spray is less of an inhalation hazard.

SAFETY
- Waterglass is mildly caustic, so gloves or regular hand-washing is indicated.
- While it's liquid, it is still silica, and bad for the lungs; if you decide to spray it, wear a mask.
- Be careful of overspray and drips, as the stuff will mar glass surfaces, and can be hard to clean off of other surfaces as well.

APPLICATION
1. Mud should be *thoroughly* dry before applying waterglass.

    Waterglass, clay, sand, and water make a gel before drying out completely. Perhaps because of the very binding properties that make it useful, it can take some time for that final drying to occur. If additional moisture is still moving out from deep in the wall, applying waterglass too soon may further slow drying.

So a thick mud wall may just *appear* to be dry. If you apply waterglass too soon, and then get rain, you may end up with soft, jelly-like patches that can even slough off completely. If you're not sure, better to let an earthen wall dry completely – a year, if need be – before waterglassing.

2. Let the waterglassed surface dry slowly.

Say you waterglass a dry wall on a sunny day. The next day you find it covered with white powder. Some of it brushes off easily, but some sticks and gives your final color an annoying dusty finish.

I've heard two explanations: one is that fast drying pulls both water and waterglass out at such a rate that the mineral ends up drying on the surface where it turns into powder; the other explanation is that the waterglass displaces other salts that may be present, and those get deposited on the surface. Either way, the problem seems to be exacerbated by overly quick drying. I waterglass late in the day after the sun is low and the heat has dropped.

LETTERS CUT IN CLAY AND CAST IN CONCRETE

An incarcerated young man cut these letters in clay for a cast concrete "freedom bench" at Hillcrest Correctional Facility, Oregon. Note the clasped hands in the middle of the "S" in "RESPECT."

CASTING STORIES IN STONE
KIKO DENZER,

The first rule for using Portland cement should be "DON'T!" The environmental cost – energy used, toxicity of byproducts (and perhaps of the material itself) – is *immense*.

Yet it is one of the most common construction materials. (For a brief review of it's applicability as a surface treatment for mud sculpture, see pages 22-23.) It's also, generally, *ugly!*

However, since it takes on the shape and texture of whatever it comes into contact with, mud can be used as a beautiful, if superficial poultice. Use it (or clay) to sculpt shape, texture, and pattern into your concrete form, or mold.

Earthen (clay-sand) plasters are ideal for texture and design on large jobs, where you have to work a big area fast.

Pure pottery clay is better for sculpting precise shapes, letters, etc. on smaller objects like benches or cast sculpture.

More examples follow on the next couple of pages.

HAND-DECORATED, MUD & CONCRETE STEMWALL

Above, at Intaba's Kitchen, we trowelled simple designs into wet mud on wood forms. When firm (but not dry) we poured concrete. We power-washed the mud off and applied rusty red stain (ferric nitrate or ferrous sulfate – both sold as fertilizer or moss-killer)

FREEDOM BENCHES

Sculpting a rose in relief requires creating an illusion of roundness on a flat surface only an inch deep. This young artist at the Hillcrest Correctional Institute in Salem, Oregon, worked quietly for a while and then said, "this sucks."

A nearbye adult tried reassuring denial: "oh, no, it's great!"

He seemed unconvinced. He had high standards, a discerning eye, and considerable skill, but this was a first effort and I think he didn't appreciate the difficulty of his task. I asked him what he didn't like.

He described the difference between a real rose and his attempt to represent it in a half inch of clay. We talked about the difference between relief sculpture and fully 3-dimensional work. Then he finished the piece without complaint, and we cast it into a concrete bench where it made an appealing design (above). One of the hardest assumptions to offset, in teaching art, is the

idea that an artist must like everything s/he makes. If you learn something from every effort, it's art.

His was just one of the many stories that went into two benches that we made to celebrate the fencing of the jail compound. Ugly and imposing as it was, the 2-story chain link fence meant that inmates could spend time outdoors. Our design process started with a silent survey of the site, followed by writing exercises and a brainstorming session. The theme of "freedom" was nearly unanimous – almost every piece of writing told how the grass and trees made the writer feel free or happy.

MORE STORIES CAST IN STONE:

Winter Gregg Kleimer and I worked with a group of boys to write stories about journeys and translate them into symbols and designs. The split concrete obelisk made a gateway into a spiral path of similarly cast stepping stones. The whole thing transformed an unused greenspace into social space.

We rolled out clay, cut letters and designs into it, set them into molds (backwards), and poured cement. The clay was sprayed or brushed with vegetable oil, to make it release more easily.

BEAUTY UN-CENSORED

Administrative staff were going to prohibit display of any art that included censored words with gang connotations, such as "wild," "magic," and "chaos," but changed their minds when they read the stories and saw the finished work. Confidentiality policies at the center prohibit identification of the artists.

SECTION FOUR

MAKING ART, (CONT'D): HOW THINGS GOT DONE

*Earthen plaster wall-hangings: seed/
vesica (above), allium (opposite); from the
catalog, Earth Art, by the author (Hand
Print Press, 2004)*

SLINGING MUD CONTINUED FROM PAGE 11
SCHOOL MURALS, KIKO DENZER

The Basotho murals are part of an agricultural tradition. The women call their work litema, from a Sesotho word meaning "to cultivate."* So I showed the students photos of Basotho houses and Karl Blossfeldt's photos of plants, as well as other natural forms, and talked to them about art, culture, and "cultivation."

Our design technique was modeled directly on the African work, which is also based on mirror images that rotate around a common center, but our drawings came out of our Pacific Northwest culture: forests, fish, flowers, etc. I selected designs to fit the space and framed the entry (see Section 2, page 33 ff). At both schools, drawing and practice panels took about a week; the murals were done with small teams, and took about three days each.

*Van Wyk, African Painted Houses, p. 78

In addition to drawings, every artist made a practice tile using earthen pigments (mud) on a 12x12 inch sheetrock panel, and a popsicle stylus for scratching designs into mud.

Chapman Hill artists documented the work and produced an illustrated booklet: "The artist...gave us pencils without erasers, that he sharpened with a knife. We made a big picture of mountains, rivers, forests, fish and plants. We made mini mirror images of the same things."

Chapman Hill
Staff, photo

After drawing and doing design exercises with 300-500 kids, there are only a few days to finish the mural, so I ask for a few small teams to work with. How the rest of the project goes depends on the artists. I try to have them do as much of the actual work as possible, but I do step in to move things along. Every project has been different; I learn as I go.

I selected individual designs and made them into a composition, but the artists had a chance to scale-up their drawings from small to large. Dividing paper (and mud) "frames" into proportional grids is an old technique that's easy to teach and learn.

Below, we're mixing a batch of mud plaster on a tarp. The white stuff is cattail fluff – the fine fiber adds strength and prevents cracking – it's easier to add it to the water, though, and then add the "fluffy" water to the sand-soil mixture. You can also use chopped straw, etc. (see "mud recipes," p. 52 ff)

When Chapman Hill Principal Patty Hoffert came out to watch kids throw mud at her school, she said, "Kiko, you have no idea how this terrifies me." It was her school, but she still had to keep district maintenance staff happy. Lead teacher Janice Wergler and groundswoman Juanita Horst helped the muddy guy contain the chaos outside her front door. It helps to have at least one on-site project champion, cheer-leader, and go-between. Parent volunteers are also a great help.

PATTERNS, "GROUP ART" & BEAUTY

We start with observation and drawing from life. Every one makes their own pattern using the same techniques — an excellent, cooperative way to develop a visual theme and composition. Every artist can identify their own (direct or indirect) part in the process. It produces stunning work, and the inherent geometry can improve the space by identifying and clarifying entrances and paths.

VOLUNTEER HANDS CONTINUED FROM PAGE 25
JAMIE TOPPER

*Bundling cattail reed thatch in Chicago's No. Park Village Nature Center,
Jamie Topper, photo*

We designed according to a list of what materials we might
harmlessly harvest at the site. We dug clay nearby, and bought
straw from a local farm. Sand was delivered cheap. Posts and
crossbeams for the shelter were buckthorn, a local invasive
that the Center is trying to eradicate. Cattail from the wet-
land provided thatch for the roof. After the first winter we
applied a lime-sand-aloe plaster, which we frescoed with
mineral pigments.

The form itself was inspired by nature center volunteers, who
handed fellow sculptor Genine Coleman and I their heartfelt
sentiments about a precious collaboration between people

and nature in a very urban environment. They are reclaiming a 40 acre former tuberculosis sanitarium by restoring native landscapes and species — the only one of its kind within city limits. To celebrate this formidable love patrol of volunteers, we symbolificized them into a growing bulb shape, with 'petals' made of countless caring hands. (The hands opened when a heavy, wet cob overhang "shplooged" off.) The foundation is hand-hewn granite pavers from an old road. They were discovered when the director of the center asked some inner city teens, "where do you go to get away from the city?" They took him to what they called "the Amazon," or "bubbly creek," a place of foul smells, sick trees, broken glass, debris — our foundation stones — and also meandering trails and a river where the black crowned night heron makes a nest.

Another story had to do with two rambunctious local boys who were assigned community service at the park. One day the director noticed them out by the sculpture. When they realized they were being watched, they knelt down in faux prayer, an instant association that the piece was some kind of mysterious holy thing. We also hear of a lot of surprise at the sculpture's structural stability, some interest in the material, and very positive feelings of sacredness. Recently, the City formally acknowledged our work with a check for 450 hours of work — delightful encouragement from the City's Department of the Environment! Our allies among the staff, especially Director Drew Hart, were a great joy, as was just about every one I got to know in this incredible community.

*Children & parents built the "fat squirrel" in 4 days, in 2000.
The floral camouflage and peace sign were added after 9/11.*

BERLIN CONTINUED FROM PAGE 17

TEN YEARS OF EARTHEN
PLAYGROUND ARCHITECTURE

TEXT & PHOTOS BY RAINER WARZECHA

What I appreciate most in this work is the quality of life that you gain working in nature. Learning from each other, giving our next generations positive work experiences, acting out creative and physical activities – these are a basic value sometimes forgotten in the modern world.

Here in our clay model of society, work can be a joyful game, the place has a positive energy, and, in my opinion, we benefit from a sparkling beam of the Lord's eye.

Our first go, from 1990-94, was just based on the wish to do. Christoph Böhm, my partner at that time, used flexible rattan sticks. I was inspired to make big things (murals, wood or metal sculptures) and had collaborated with several artists working in these fields. We called that early clay village 'Makunaima,' after a South American mythical figure who, as a grown adult, represents the wisdom of childhood.

The sculpting of 'earth-heads' and other ephemeral structures continued for 5 years, and evolved with publicity and

Here are pictures of our clay village, 'Makunaima,' which has been changing shape for years, but has now found a permanent form. The name comes from an indigenous South American story about a man who teaches people by acting the part of the clever child.

In Berlin, Rainer's largest ensemble of earthen sculptures is located in Britzer Garten, south of Berlin's center.

A 12th century Saxon named Albert the Bear gave Berlin her totem animal, recreated here, in mud, in 2002.

participation. In 1998 a huge final festival of ephemeral building in Weil der Stadt drew more than 3000 participants. After that, we started to build more permanent structures, and a real village.

MAKUNAIMA – THE CLAY VILLAGE PROJECT IN BERLIN'S BRITZER GARDEN

'Makunaima' started about 14 years ago as a 'leisure-activity' for the 6 week German summer holidays, and has become a living organism, a real 'clay village' that grows and changes. It began with caves of mud, like the "primitive" but already elaborately architectural African clay hut. Medieval, Mayan, and Indian styles provided inspiration, as did big minds like

Weil der Stadt brought out 3300 kids, teachers, and helpers who built for two weeks in May, 1998.

Antonio Gaudi. Concrete provided foundations, but what made the buildings singular was the visible touch of hands, and the experience of earthen buildings of a style not usually seen in the city.

Everything built before 1996 is gone now, except a desk made of stone in the center of the old village. We had to learn how to build and we had nearly no money for materials. Just earth, wire, sticks, and some color. Now the situation has improved, but there is still a charm of poverty in it.

Financing was an annual challenge, but as the project made more and more friends, it made itself irreplaceable. I was lucky to find sponsors and helping hands. The crew grew, bringing together craftsmen, teachers and artists, all working for small wages but inspired by the positive feedback and happiness of our young partners, who were and are a rich source of fun and joy. On a regular day, we had 30-40 kids working with us; some days up to 100 would show up.

As we progressed, I wanted our sculptures to be resistant and more permanent. I wanted to add huts and houses and to make our 'clay-village' a reality. I studied, traveled, learned from others. Every season I tried to improve plasters and

Many hands helped build the palace of fun (spielpalast). Here the children sieve clay for a finish plaster. Some came year after year. Opposite, top: an early "earth head;" below: Rainer at work on the bear sculpture, which was roughed out with mud bricks.

finishes on the sculptures. I developed a more architectural approach, but I needed help on a professional scale from different points of view.

The 'pope' of German clay building, Gernot Minke, recommended a product from BASF, a polymer that helped us build walls that resisted rain and impact. And, in negotiations with my partners, I insisted on good foundations under the new structures.

Just beneath the 'Makunaima' clay-village was another spot where old playground structures were being removed. I was asked about my visions for the area, and convinced the authorities to give us the space for building and to invest in higher construction standards.

In 2003, we built the 'Spielpalast' ('palace of fun') – which mixed concrete, metal, stone, wood, and clay. It was the visible sign of a new approach from all sides. Then in 2004 we began to build a labyrinth of clay, stone, and wood, also using glass-mosaic (in concrete) on top of earthen walls.

The work has become more diverse, involving adults in more expert activities, and offering children a range of activities. The younger ones prefer to play and do tiny projects in the clay village; older kids want to be part of the serious building stuff. And the lead team needs time to apply their expertise to the building. Nevertheless 'Makunaima' is still a group project, with a high level of interaction between adults and children.

BUILDING OF SPIELPALAST (JULY-OCTOBER, '03)

Spielpalast combines an octopus-sculpture (made from concrete finished with glass mosaic), an earthen tower and a

middle part connecting both elements. The earthen construction was linked to the 'Makunaima' event during summer holidays, which brought in lots of helping hands.

The octopus sculpture required 8 tons of concrete around a steel form, and a specialist team helped us build a strong foundation. Ivan, a carpenter on my team, built the

The construction of the "Palaver-pavillon" (Pavilion of united cultures).

The 'Spielpalast' ('palace of fun'): concrete, metal, stone, wood and clay. The octopus-sculpture is concrete and mosaic, the tower is mud-brick, as are the walls connecting the two. The mosaic contained 8000 tiny bits of colored glass, each one cut and fit in place.

roof. Children from 'Makunaima 03' helped with the 2300 mud-bricks that went into the project that summer — one of the hottest and driest in decades.

After finishing the octopus, we spent two intensive weeks making the mosaic on top of the concrete body. A few selected helpers, (some children among them), helped cut 8,000 tiny bits of colored glass!

It all took about 2000 hours of work , as well as sponsorship from Claytec, BASF, and a local housing company that donated the slide.

Top: an apprentice mud-mason helps lay some of the 2300 mud-bricks that went into the tower and walls of the Spielpalast. The hottest and driest summer in decades helped speed the work. Below: another view of the tower. (A "mason," by the way, is a "maker." Both words come from the same root.)

DESIGNING THE MAKUNAIMA & BERLIN PROJECTS

BY RAINER WARZECHA

The designs for the sculptures and houses come from my drawings, or sometimes from my partners. Some details are linked to the process. What material is cheap? What looks best? Brainstorming with co-workers or children, or our general mood also initiates the creative process. I like to leave some 5-10 percent open, when it comes to the final touch. As I'm working with artists, I want to let them participate in the design, and be creative as long as they follow the main line of the building plan.

Design decisions are based on the team. We discuss aspects of a certain detail. If technical refinement is needed, if it's 'in tune' with my inner vision, or if a team member has a good solution, then we do it. Children generally initiate or accompany our 'mindflow' with comments and wishes. In case of doubt or differences, I have to decide. I also work from sketches and architectural designs.

In the first years we were more spontaneous. For example, the children wanted to have a prison. We quickly built one, and it was great to play 'cops and robbers.' Or I let the kids make small models and the group decided which to build.

I also try to feel the energy of the surroundings. Following basic feng shui pays off. It's not possible to put a thing any place, without referring to the energies and social relations there. If the location 'speaks to me,' I plan accordingly.

Painting and final decoration is mostly done by the artists involved. We select some talented boys and girls to support us. Mostly the designs follow an agreed upon plan, with

more freedom in the details. In the end it's like playing music together. You are free to play, but try to play in tune! I try to give a visual bass-line or melody that the others can relate to, and allow for solos and/or interpretation.

Especially on the Makunaima project, we tried to let it grow slowly, by working together with visitors and kids who come to play. It helps to have a good team with confidence in each other.

Our 'leading vision' is more or less, the 'spirit of aliveness.' If I didn't love the project, which gives me a lot of positive energy, I wouldn't have the will to go on with it (especially Makunaima). In general, it's my way of art, inspiring people to do something extraordinary, as I know how rewarding and beneficial these processes are.

Working together makes things and hearts grow together. In the villages of the Maya Indians it is a normal thing, that neighbours – yea, the whole village - help each other; if a young couple decides to build a house to live in, everybody tries to support them. We have lost a lot of these values...

But looking towards Asia after the Tsunami and the amount of aid that is offered shows that a certain impulse of that kind of 'one world consciousness' is growing again - even in a bigger scale. We will need it in the future!

his back yard, using sticks and plastic and other recycled materials that cost nothing.

Some neighbors warmed to the invitation; others watched. Mostly, people liked it and made it a neighborhood social spot. After several months, however, Mark realized that it wasn't quite right for a private building to be the *center* of a neighborhood. Even a funky tea-house was still private space – still a bar against public entry. Only a truly public space would be open. But the only public space was the intersection up the street. Mark says "the jump from T-Hows to Public Square took 3 months to begin, with a 2 month overlap until the T-Hows closed...two weeks later the intersection was in full bloom."

It started when Mark asked one of the neighbors on the intersection for permission to build a 24-hour T-station on her corner. There was no "design," just a post with a shelf for a thermos of hot water and a honey bear; cups on nails, sheltered by a small roof of scrap plastic. Anne Marie contributed decorations, and it was done in a couple of hours. People used it.

Mark planted sunflowers and corn on 3 corners, and a month and a half later there was living wall of color around the intersection. On the 4th corner, however, lived Brian, a "giant, Viking sized auto mechanic who wouldn't have anything to do with us," says Mark. Until a beautiful young neighbor named Emily got involved. One warm day she knocked on Brian's door wearing a string bikini, to ask about building something on his corner, too.

Brian saw the tactic for what it was – and said "OK."

But the intersection was still an intersection, a place for cars. Some kids (and adults) who used the sidewalk for drawing chalk patterns during gatherings sowed the idea for the first foray into the intersection itself. Mark remembers: "Here we were in a crossroads, but it wasn't working, there's was no *here* here." Instead of inviting peole *in* to the crossroads,

THE MEMORIAL LIFEHOWS

SE 37th & Taylor, commemorates the life of Matt Sheckel, a bicyclist who was killed by a truck here. The Transportation Safety Committee teamed with Matt's mother, Marsha, and City Repair to build a sacred place. The all-weather cob pillar features photovoltaic systems so it glows at night. Joseph Kennedy was the lead builder, working with several dozen neighbors and friends of Matt's. It was finished in ten days, in May of 2002. (mL Photo)

SUNNYSIDE PIAZZA KIOSK

SE 33rd & Yamhill, another cob structure, with a living roof and photovoltaics that light the interior at night. Over ten days, Robert Bolman and Sukita Crimmell led over a hundred neighbors and friends in the building of this structure, as well as a sculptural sixty foot-long cob-faced retaining wall, and a solar powered water fountain with mosaic glass details. (mL photo)

CITY BIKES COLLECTIVE

8th & Ankeny, SE Portland, 2003 Village Building Convergence. On the bench are the core team who took the project to completion. On the left is a shrine to the Virgen de Guadelupe, patron saint of Mexico. Down the street is a pick-up site for (mostly Mexican) day laborers, some of whom joined the team or helped out. The central table features a mosaic of bike gears and parts. A bike-frame awning was added later. The bench seats are wood.

the intersection (and the cars) kept them out. Mark thought they needed to claim the intersection itself as public space. He wrote up the idea, presented it, and everyone said yes.

Over a weekend, as part of an impromptu block party, they painted a huge mandala in the middle of the intersection. Cars had to wait for people. Some complained. That brought out the authorities, who did what authorities do, and ordered the "unpermitted activities" to stop. (Mark suggests that the complaints came from residents of an upscale condominium several blocks away who only experienced the intersection from their cars — for them, convenience came before community.)

But it was too much for those involved to just "stop": too much momentum from too many people whose lives were too much enlarged by each other's company. So they went with Mark to City Hall, to champion their newly defined public space.

DIGNITY VILLAGE

NE Portland, is part of a self-help community by and for homeless people.
Lydia Doleman, Chris Sobreto, and Sean McDonnell led over 400 people, including resident Villagers, in building five beautiful strawclay houses over the ten-day span of a 2004 Village Building Convergence. Villagers plan to build more. (mL photo)

Councillors expecting a fight were taken off guard by Mark's "friendly but persistent" approach. Buttressed by his own neighbors, he treated each person as another neighbor waiting for the right invitation to join the party.

"The legal transformation took about three months to begin," he recalls, "from installation through dialogue and stalling tactics. Then city hall was engaged, the intersection was safe, and then it took another three months to work out the ordinance. So, I would say it took three months to get city hall up to speed and with us." After that, the city went on to draft a new ordinance creating a legal basis for neighbors all over Portland to "repair" their own intersections.

Years before, a wise man had told Mark that "words won't get you anywhere."

"So I set about to do something. I didn't know what it was, but I couldn't talk about it. I just had to do it."

This article was written by Kiko Denzer, based on an interview and correspondence with Mark Lakeman.

who all lived in the same community.

They sketched designs, mixed mud, gathered materials, and developed stories and characters. Plans and plots changed as relationships grew; landscaping filled the model "sites." Their village was displayed for a public unveiling and reading. Such hands-on building, combined with writing and storytelling, engaged them in real maturation and learning. Cooperation required real thought and caring.

From looking inward at themselves, in a mirror provided by adults, they had to look outward at tangible work and a shared goal. With a shift in focus came a shift in behavior. Participation, at least in part, became it's own reward. Some declared intentions to build real houses. Others broke silence to speak, share, and smile. Several overcame "I can't do it" fears, and made structures of which they were rightly proud (including several marvelous, and carefully thatched roofs).

"HOME IS..."

"...where you feel comfortable and accepted." — Michal B.

"a warm and cozy place..." — Josh P.

"...comfortable and it keeps you warm and safe." — Michael D.

"where you are yourself." — Lucas R.

"a place to turn to for warmth." — Justin F.

"...free your body and mind, find your way home." — Andy B.

All but the bottom photo are from a project at the Corvallis (OR) Farm Home. Note the wonderful roof solutions. All the roofing and decorative materials were scrounged on site. We had to dig holes for mud elsewhere.

Below, the results of a one day, impromptu village-building session that was part of a community art project in a low-income housing development in Newport, Oregon. The other piece was a falcon oven.

4. Roof material (shingles, shakes, plywood, old tin, glued together CDs, giant tree mushrooms, flower pot trays, old cans).
5. A tube or sleeve (a section of rubber hose).
6. Coat hangers and a thin, rot-resistant stick.
7. Daub material (MUD! see page 60).
8. TOOLS: wood saws, a drill and bits, and, if you don't want to mix by foot, a 5 gallon bucket and a half inch drill with four inch drywall mixing paddle (or a heavy duty 3/8 inch drill and 2 inch paint mixer).

12 STEPS TO A BIRDHOUSE:

1. Cut a 5 1/2 inch diameter base.
2. Drill seven 1/4 inch holes, in a circle, equally spaced & 1/4 inch from the edge of your base (to hold the wattle uprights). The number is odd so that the pattern alternates: over and under. Note: the first base can be a template for multiples.)

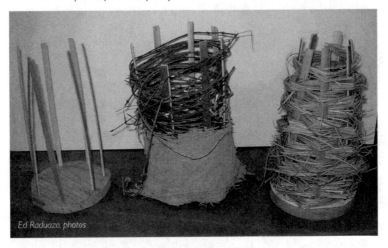

Ed Raduazo, photos

3. Prepare the vertical sticks; each one should be a bit wider than its hole.
4. Insert 7 vertical sticks in 7 holes.
5. Weave.
6. Fill a 5-gallon bucket 3/4 full of clay soil, add water and mix. Press it through a 1/4 inch screen to remove rocks. Window screen makes even finer plaster.
7. Add fine fiber: paper pulp, cattail fluff, dryer lint, or "urban straw" – in

our case, shredded documents from the US Patent & Trademark Office.

8. Apply daub (I dip my 'straw' in the clay, swish it around 'til coated, then squeegee most of the clay off). Overlapping the layers makes them stronger.
9. Form the entry hole.
10. Add the stabilizing bar (a wooden stick put through the wall about 3/4 of the way up — see photos on page 31).

11. Attach coat hangers and roof.
12. To attach bird house to base, bend coat hanger into a "J," run it through the stabilizer and hook it into the base (much easier after the mud has dried).

LABYRINTHS & DIALS CONTINUED FROM PAGE 21

MAKE A LABYRINTH, MEASURE THE EARTH

The best way to understand the labyrinth is to try the geometry, a word which means "earth measure" – which is what drawing really is!

Diagram 1 is the "seed" for the design. Diagram 2 illustrates how the seed grows into the "circuits" of the labyrinth. This one has seven circuits (you can try a simple four circuit labyrinth by making a seed from a "plus" sign (+) with dots in a square pattern at the corners between the arms. Connect one dot to the neighboring end of the cross, and the next pair, and the next.... Try making up seeds of your own....)

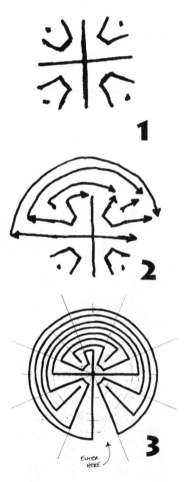

1

2

3

Trace the path in diagram 3 – it doesn't lead to the center of the circle. Let your eye look with your mind quiet. What do you notice? Do you see light and dark? changes in direction? pattern? Connect the corners where the paths turn, and you'll see two spirals that meet exactly at the heart of the labyrinth! (diagram next page.) Together, they form a heart!

Our seed pattern begins with a cross in the circle. Every step out from the intersection of that cross, our circle gets bigger and it takes more steps to go 'round.

BEAUTIFUL !

SPIRAL PATHS !

The spiral marks the relationship between growth (each step further from the center) and form (the area enclosed by the bigger circle). Growth is not a linear measure, but the paths and shapes we make as we learn.

The cross is where vertical meets horizontal; the circle is the whole; the spiral is the living connection between them. It is a labyrinth in itself.

Spirals occur in shells, in the pattern of seeds in a sunflower, in the whorls of fingerprints and the whorls of galaxies. The Pythagoreans of Greece observed (in the 6th century B.C.) that one of the most common relationships between growth and form – or one of the most common spirals – could be described mathematically as a ratio of 13 to 21. They called it "the Golden Mean."

It is perhaps easiest to understand by drawing a series of squares that grow, like a cell, by doubling.

One plus one is two – two squares, side by side, each 1x1. They grow out from their long side to make a third square of dimension 2x2. But now, rather than doubling, we add the last dimension to the one before, 1 + 2 = 3. The process continues by squaring the long side of the rectangle to make a new rectangle of the same proportion.

So we get sets of rectangles, 3x5, 5x8, 8x13, etc. It is a famous series of numbers. Leonardo of Pisa introduced it to Europe 800 years ago (along with arabic numbers and the decimal system). For his contribution, they called the series by his nickname, "Fibonacci."

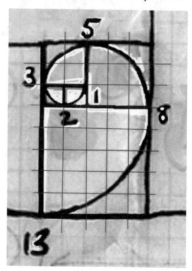

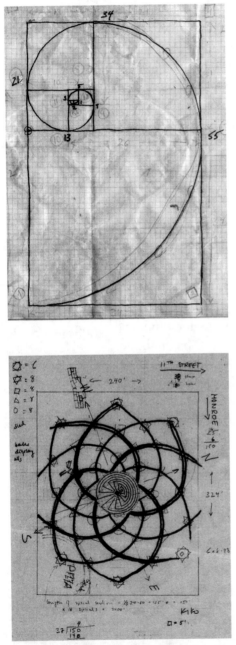

The Greeks called the Fibonacci rectangle "golden" because *every* Fibonacci pair (after 13) makes a ratio of 1.618, or .618. The relationship of one Fibonacci number to the next is so constant in nature that it was understood as a principle of divine harmony and proportion.

We find Fibonacci series and the golden mean in the shapes and sizes of flowers, shells, galaxies, human bodies and many works of human art. The labyrinth combines those rational and irrational elements in a way that we can appreciate visually, and experience physically. That's beautiful!

*Top: a Fibonacci spiral.
Bottom: Plan for extending the spiral theme of a labyrinth out into the surrounding space. We used bamboo poles to hold plastic ribbons spiralling overhead.*

BEGIN A LABYRINTH OR DIAL DESIGN BY FINDING THE FOUR DIRECTIONS

This geometry exercise locates true north and the four directions; it can also give you a physical experience of the movement of the earth — as well as orienting your structures.

Begin on a sunny morning. Put a stick in the ground. It should be straight up and down – use a plumb bob or a spirit level. Make a rude compass with string and a funnel filled with flour or sand. Make a generous loop at one end of the string and drop it over the stick; it should move freely. Stretch the string out until it's as long as the shadow of the stick. Loop that end around the bottom of the funnel so you can draw a sand-circle with a radius as long as the shadow of the stick. Mark the place on the circle where the shadow touches.

WATCH THE SHADOW

Almost immediately, you'll see it pull back from your circle. As the hours pass, it will shrink more, and then start to grow again. Finally, it will touch the circle again. Get ready! Just when it touches the circle, make a mark. Draw a line from mark to mark. That line is your east/west axis — the direction of the sun as it appears to move through the day.

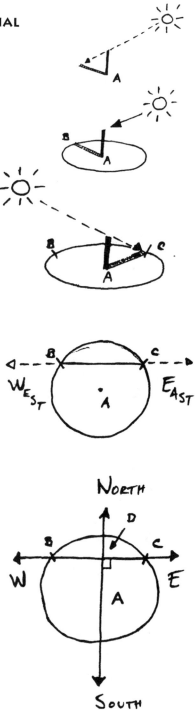

PLANNING YOUR LABYRINTH

Practice drawing a few labyrinths on paper first (see exercise on page 100). Then measure your drawings. This design (there are many) has seven major circuits, or paths, plus two minor ones and a space at the intersection of the cross. It's important to leave room at the end so people (and wheelchairs!) can pass.

So, 2 foot paths, multiplied by 9 circuits (7+2), plus 2 feet for extra space at the center. Call it 3x9 – 27 feet – that was the radius of our circle. (use graph paper to work it all out on a small scale.)

SLICE YOUR PIE IN EQUAL PIECES

To divide the pie into sixteen equal pieces, as shown here, start with a cross; divide each quadrant into four; draw straight lines between the ends of your radii, find the centers, and draw a new set of radii, dividing your quarter circles in half, etc., OR,
- divide the circumference ($2\pi r$) by 16 and mark off the segments with a tape, OR
- divide 360° by 16 and use a compass, or
- use trigonometry (sin, cos, tan) to find the length of the side opposite the angle.

DRAW CIRCULAR CIRCUITS

Think of the central cross as a body: the vertical line is head and trunk, the horizontal line is two arms. (Where you start and whether you connect lines to the right or left makes the labyrinth right or left-handed.) Starting at the head, each radial line has to be longer than the last by the width of your pathway. Use a tape and stakes to measure and locate where each of your 16 radial lines must end. Starting at the head, connect the ends of the lines. Use a rope or other makeshift "compass" to connect them; and keep your rope taught and your marker vertical. (See the photos of the construction process.)

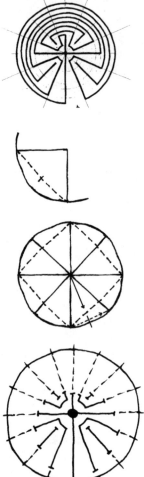

STEP BY STEP

On a 60 foot square tarp of donated lumber wrap, we drew out a full size labyrinth with a "compass" made of a rope and a grease marker on a stick. It was a mistake to draw on the black side because when we spread it out on the ground, it concentrated the sun's heat and scorched the grass.

With tarp as our template, we drilled holes about a foot apart along every circuit. Then we removed the tarp, and inserted alder, hazel, and vine maple poles into the holes. Two big columns marked the entry; a third marked the intersection of the central cross, the "sacred home of elder brother Itoi."

Vertical sticks had been cut and pre-sorted by length so the walls of each succeeding circuit dropped in height as you moved inward.

Just a single pair of long hazel or vine maple "withies," woven over and under the vertical poles, made the "walls" very stable & strong. On the outermost circuit we wove an ample panel on which to make bas-relief sculpture.

Columns were made of bamboo lath; 12" plywood disks with scalloped edges, on either end of a 2x4, provided structure on which to lash the bamboo.

Each column frame was guyed to the ground, plastered with mud, and then painted with colored earths: white, yellow, and red.

White doves were released for the finale of an original chorale written for the occasion and performed by the local peace choir.

Thousands walked the path and visited the village space it created during the two and half day festival. Passers-by contributed spontaneous bas-relief sculpture to the outer wall.

The pathways were wide enough so you could "walk the labyrinth" in a wheelchair too.

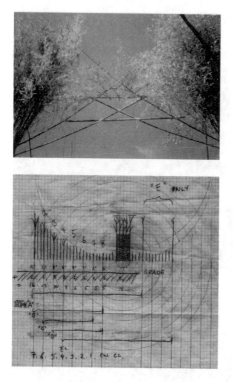

BEGINNINGS & ENDS

The design started on paper, and included a scale model, but we made improvements along the way – as when Jan said, "the gateway needs something," and lashed leftover bamboo into this pediment. Local school kids made cloth banners that we hung around the outside.

Volunteers numbered about 200, many from a local church which provided support and coordination; many others turned out on the spur of the moment.

We took it down a week later, in a matter of hours. The mud & bamboo columns went to someone's garden in a pickup truck; the sticks became firewood for the next winter (amazing volume of wood in a few hundred skinny sticks!) But all those feet left a labyrinth in the grass that people continued to walk for weeks.

construction photos: Molly Mondoux and Ann Wiseman.

MAKE A MUD-DIAL

Sundial construction began the same way the labyrinth did, by finding true north to orient the framework of the gnomon. I used basic trigonometry (sin, cosine, tangent) to make sure that the gnomon was also at the right angle, which had to be equal to our latitude in Corvallis, Oregon (44 degrees and 34 minutes).

After framing the gnomon, we drew out the ellipse for the base, lined it halfway with bales, and called in the dump trucks. One of the drivers was so skilled he could pour out a 16" deep strip of sand almost precisely to the line. The other one left irregular piles we had to spread by hand.

Once the framing was secure in the sand base, we lashed on a gridwork of bamboo, and covered that with cardboard, also lashed and stapled.

We mixed mud on tarps, with as many people as wanted to get muddy. For applying mud to the gnomon structure, we borrowed a trick from earthen builders in Africa, who build scaffolding right into the structure itself: much cheaper than ladders and heavy steel platforms, and more fun than a jungle gym — not to mention the unusual look.

SUNDIALS TELL MORE THAN TIME

A sundial not only tells time, it also translates the grand celestial story of sun and earth into something small and easy for humans to understand. Geometry (literally, "earth-measure") is the language of translation.

The *gnomon* is the part of the dial that throws the shadow and indicates the hour. The word is related to "narrate" and "notify" by a Greek root meaning "to know."

In the diagram, you'll see that that the dial face is

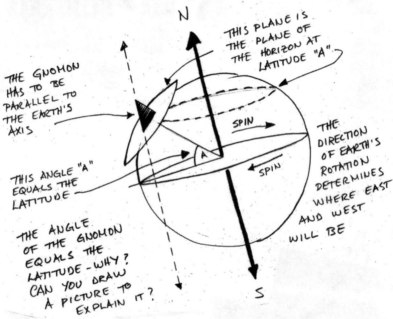

tilted, while the gnomon is parallel to the axis of the earth. The tilt of the gnomon means that dial *and* planet always have the same orientation to the sun. That sameness of orientation is what makes it possible for the dial to tell time.

But it also makes the dial a model of our relationship to the whole sky. For example, in the northern hemisphere, the earth's axis (and the gnomon) point to the North Star. So dial becomes compass, locating you in relation to the four directions, *and* the starry sky. In addition, you can use the dial to tell you what season it is by marking the length of the noon shadow through the year. And since the seasons are caused by the relative position of sun and earth, you know something more about your relationship to the sky.

So the dial tells many stories: how earth is related to sun, how earth and sun are related to the stars, and how each tiny person can be connected to it all — amazing!

If you'd like to make a sundial, there are many books that will show you how (including a little companion volume to this one), as well as websites — see the resource section for info).

INTRODUCTION & AFTERWORD: ART *IS...*

Art is many things, but here what I mean by "art" is that kind of experience by which humans learn.

Working with mud, sand, and straw is a way to teach geology, engineering, physics, history, drawing, composition, and design. It is also a way to teach social skills, like cooperation. But more important than just *what* it teaches is *how* it teaches:

Jon Young is a wilderness educator who takes kids into the woods, and teaches them to identify and track wildlife, among other things. He cites Microsoft research suggesting that tracks in the mud were an original source of writing, that alphabets are like birdprints, and that *reading* a set of tracks, from a brain science point of view, is the same as reading a bunch of symbols written on a page in ink.

He also says the kids who do best are those labelled "ADD," or "Attention Deficit Disorder," who are too wound up to sit still, but who can develop total focus on a set of tracks because the tracks *require* them to move. The excellence they develop for this *kinetic* reading reliably transfers into the classroom, where their grades

Desiree designed this pig oven as part of a youth garden project in Corvallis, Oregon. It's used regularly for garden pizza parties and fundraisers.

improve. Young concludes that kids don't have "learning disorders," *schools* have *teaching* disorders.*

As an occasional "artist-in-residence" in schools and other public settings, I've come to much the same conclusion. I gave one second grade class some simple drawing exercises. All the kids set to work. I stood back and watched, waiting for the rare question. The teacher stood next to me appreciatively, and asked if she could make some copies of the exercises. "The only time they're ever this quiet is when we do art," she said.

I was too stunned to ask the obvious question: *"why not do more art?"* But it occurs to me now that part of the problem is that art is treated as a separate subject, rather than as a *method.*

As method, art is simply a way of learning that requires greater physical involvement than reading and writing. And while it can be done at a desk, it gains force with greater involvement.

For example: at a treatment center for at-risk youth, I and the writer working with me were warned that it was "one of those days," and we might have to cut short our session due to behavior problems. We were building a model village, out of earth. The kids had drawn designs for their houses, developed stories about the characters who lived in them, mixed mud, and roughed out the homes on 2x2 foot pieces of plywood. Only finish work remained.

The kids lined up, single file, military formation, for the hundred yard silent walk to our "shop." An extra adult or two (for a total of 4 or 5) ensured adequate supervision for 7 kids.

They arrived and set to work in palpable quiet and concentration. Gregg and I attended occasional calls for help or materials, or technical discussions about design and engineering. One of the most sullen kids volunteered a positive remark.

Staff were amazed at what seemed to them a remarkable transformation. I was amazed that what was obvious to me seemed hidden to them: we were engaging the students in something *outside themselves.* Rather than trying to "control negative behaviors" we had engaged them in a positive, collaborative effort to achieve a shared goal.

Unfortunately, in the field of public health, and as a socio-economic category, "youth" is often associated with disease, and not just in "treatment centers." Violence, drugs, alcohol abuse, and fear are daily fare at school, and even healthy kids who exhibit "negative behaviors" are evaluated to see if they're "at risk," as though early diagnosis will prevent infection.

It seems to me that art, as a method, is a healthier preventative that accepts reality as it is rather than trying to deny it. Finding and claiming beauty, which can be done even in the midst of war, is a fundamentally positive act that helps unite a fragmented world, and makes sense of harsh and confusing realities.

As Wendell Berry writes: "When all the parts of the body are working together, are under each other's influence, we say that it is whole; it is healthy. The same is true of the world, of which our bodies are parts. The parts are healthy insofar as they are joined harmoniously to the whole...."+

Art helps join us, harmoniously, to a whole. It is a way to understand our place in the world. That it has become, too often, a rarified expression of some unique individual vision is, I think, evidence of fragmentation, not art. But if we look a bit deeper, we find art in every basic activity of everyday life.

John Wesley Powell put it another way that makes immense sense to me. He said, "the greater part of knowledge is always preceded by generations of doing."* Powell explored the Colorado River before it was tamed, and knew and respected the way that native peoples lived in harmony with land, life, and other creatures. At the start of the 20th century, he wrote that phrase to introduce Frank Hamilton Cushing's classic ethnographic study, *Zuñi Breadstuff.*

Powell called Cushing "a man of genius" because as a teenager, he had learned from indigenous sources all the skills needed to trans-

form the stuff of wilderness into the stuff of civilization — tools, vessels, shelter, clothing. His manual skill became the basis of immense scholarship, won him membership and a place of leadership in the Zuñi tribe, and made him into a teacher of future generations, a conduit for the re-creation of culture – all based on simple acts of *doing*.

By contrast, when I was a kid interested in stone-carving, I found materials in art shops and bought small chunks of cut stone off metal shelves. What I couldn't buy was a fundamental knowledge of the essential wholeness that any art tries to express: the forces and landforms that made stone and quarry, the taste and sources of water filtered by layers of ancient rock, or the human stories that linked me, my stone, chisels, and the animal shapes I made, to the rest of my world.

Though I loved the *doing* of it, "being an artist" seemed shallow and dull. "Success" meant selling stuff to strangers. The reward was just money. Artists were middlemen, trapped by things that had nothing to do with art: the "market," galleries, critics and collectors. Where was the joy of doing what I loved? Meaning and beauty? Inspiration and communication? I turned cynical, and abandoned art as cut off from people, place, beauty, *culture*.

Working with earth for the past ten years, however, has changed me. Everywhere I step is a quarry. Everywhere I dig, I build relation-

Desirée's Pig Oven, protected by the timber frame shed the kids built. Tracy Noel (left) coordinates the Corvallis Youth Garden; beside her is arts council staffer Tricia Sorgen. On the right is a devoted volunteer who loves baking in the oven.

A MANUAL FOR MAKING ART OUT OF EARTH   117

ships. The result is not sculpture or architecture, but *home:* beauty that I share by inhabiting. When ethnologists call pottery one of the first indications of human civilization they are merely naming the obvious — when we shape the earth, we shape ourselves.

I *felt* this wholeness long before I knew or began to work for it as an idea – and I had work at it for a while before I understood it. First, I started to garden, and to eat from my garden. Then I knew – by my hands – that I came from the earth. When I started to work with kids, I knew by experience that the act of *making* is more important than the thing made, *or* the maker.

Recently, a friend asked me to make a container for the ashes of her late husband, Jack. Being a sculptor and not a potter, I offered to contain the ashes in the material itself — to mix earth and ash, and make them into something that would be "beautiful to look at and friendly to live with."

She said yes, and delivered a small plastic box. Inside was a plastic bag containing a few pounds of bone-grey gritty ash. There's not much left after a body is incinerated (a process requiring thirty gallons of propane — enough, at our house, to cook our meals for 6 months!) The bulk of the tissues — primarily carbon, nitrogen, and water — all return to the air to be re-synthesized by green plants. The part that comes from the earth goes back to the earth looking alot like sand and grit.

Familiar as I am with sand and grit, this was Jack going through the screen that I used to separate coarse from fine particles. He watched me from a photo on the wall as I worked. It slowed me down. It seemed disrespectful to just let bits fall on the floor, so I was careful not to drop bits; I paid extra attention.

Materials speak. They tell you what they can and can't do. Sand varies according to the mountains it's made from, how it's worked by weather and water: rain, stream, river, or ocean. Ash has qualities too, peculiar to its sources and the river of time and technology that carries it through life and death and back to life. Jack's ashes behaved differently than sand — felt different, stuck to and pulled differently on the trowel, differed in how it came to the surface when polished, how it reflected light....

All the time, I had in mind that *this* was Jack.

Then I remembered what the red men tried to tell the white men who demanded the right to buy and own their land: *how can we sell you the bones of our fathers and mothers, the bodies of our children?* Land, people, life are all one — a gift from a generous creator, and one that finally returns to its source.

A shovel feels different now. I dig with respect; I pay attention.

William Morris suggested that the highest duty of the artist is to make a beautiful home. I don't know if he meant a house and garden, or if he meant home in the larger sense of our place on earth, but my wife and son and I share a small house in a large garden which feeds us vegetables and beauty. A few years ago, planting and fertilizing and eating out of my own garden for the first time, I realized that my purpose is to make compost — to go back to the ground that grew me. As obvious as that may seem to read, it took a couple cycles of *doing* before it became tangible enough for me to

Kids in Atlanga, Mexico, act out a spider in a game of charades that resulted in the sculpture at left.

know that my small part is worth doing, to feel the comfort and confidence that my life will have value when I die, that somehow, it will be in harmony with others – animal, plant, soil.

All of this reassures me that art is not a *thing*, it's the who and how and why of all my making: not "pieces" and exhibits and money, but children and relationships and home and family and community and neighborhood and citizenship – including taxes paid (or not, because a garden isn't taxable)....

Kathleen Norris writes that "there is but one creator, and 'creating' is the very thing that artists cannot do. The gifts of the human imagination that artists employ operate equally in science and scholarship, teaching and philosophy, business and mathematics, ranching, preaching, engineering, mothering and fathering." She goes on to suggest that the goal of art may just be for the artist to "come to a mature understanding of their communal role."++

Mud has given me a communal role, because it invites participation and

"sword fern," 12x36" earth plaster, by the author.

promises pleasure as well as beauty. By simplifying the doing of art, mud offers a direct and simple connection to wholeness – a wholeness that seems to me more durable than bronze or marble.

NOTES:
* Interview with John Young, by Christina Bertea, in *Newvillage* Magazine, no. 3, 2002, p. 60.
+ from *The Unsettling of America*
** In the Foreword to Frank Hamilton Cushing's classic exploration of Zuñi food and culture, *Zuñi Breadstuff*, Heye Foundation, 1920, p. 13-15.
++ *The Cloister Walk*, by Kathleen Norris, Riverhead Books, NY, 1997. Norris is a poet who, among other things, works as an artist-in-residence teaching poetry to children in public schools in South Dakota.

THANKS:

In schools where I've had the privilege to be "Artist-in-Residence" — and where, due to tight schedules, large numbers, and a small brain, I've had to call kids just "George" or "Martha" — to every George and Martha, thanks for helping with projects I'd never get to do on my own. May you have art teachers who know you long enough to learn your name;

To parents in PTAs who fight and pay for art education in the face of declining budgets and a "meat and potatoes" approach to curriculum development in which art is considered candy rather than vital, green vegetable or basic hearty bread;

To staff at schools and other institutions where I've worked who try to give students a varied diet, and who welcome itinerant artists: especially Marla McVay, Janice Wergler, Patty Hoffert, Juanita Horst, Brock Holt, Faye Cummins, Denise Gorthy, Julee Kopta, Chris Duval, Frieda Grier, Carol Griffith, John Bohle, Cherie Taylor, Sharon Thornagle, Jerry Shick, Carrie Kart; Catherine Johnstone;

To Oregon's regional Arts Association staff, who coordinate the state Arts-in-Education program, write grants, raise funds, organize and employ artists – in particular: Corby Stonebraker, Victoria Fridley, Mary Van Denend, Tricia Sorgen, Kim Barker, Jan Eastman, Sharon Morgan, Jane Schneider, Sara Swanberg, Bill Flood, Paula Portinga Booth, Kathy Burton, the Corvallis Arts Center, the Oregon Commission on Children & Families, and the Arts Reaching Youth program;

For all manner of support and collaboration, thanks to: Suzannah Doyle, Gregg Kleiner, Tracy Noel and the Corvallis Youth Garden, Lilliann Rosenberg, Paige and Bill Shumway, Karen Harding, Piper Jones, Nan Dudek, Charlie Bremer, Jill Lorenzini, Kyla Wetherell, Lynn Ward, Gerry Brehm, Kristi Hager, Stuart and Elizabeth, Jim Domingo, Sidney and Guli Field, Kathi Borrego, Rick Caske, John Selker, Michael Sullivan, Josie Gribskow, Bob, Jan, and Sean Blount, Gerry, Matt, Darol Streib, Pat Watkins, Sterling Grant, Dona Griffith, Hank Schroeder, Cosmo Allen, Cheryl Good, Honorio Reyes-Z., Jaap Bongers, Johanna and Hannah, Mary Goodlad, Edna Abbot, Oregon State University, Green & White Rock Products, Morse Brothers Gravel, Eichler Hay Company, Garland's Nursery, Corvallis Gazette Times, Stover, Evey, & Jackson, OSU cow barn, Denson's Feed & Seed , Unity of Corvallis, Corvallis United Methodist Church, & Corvallis Davinci Days; and all the unnamed teachers and participants who gave me pictures and whose names went unrecorded. Special thanks to Molly Mondoux for wonderful labyrinth photos;

For inspiration, encouragement, information, example, and guidance, thanks to: Ianto Evans, Linda Smiley, Michael Smith, Alejandra Caballero, Paco Gomez, Catherine Wanek & Pete Fust, Clark Sanders, Jason Saunders, Ocean and Intaba Liff-Anderson;

Thanks to Mark Lakeman, Rainer Warzecha, Jamie Topper, and Ed Raduazo for adding your stories and pictures to this effort. Thanks for the title to Arrested Development, who sing truth; on the web at www.lifemusik.com.

For Bev's way of teaching by learning, and for their combined faith in the inherent potential (and longevity) of very small seeds, thanks to Beverly Brown and Tee Corinne.

For the best part of my own education, which was her example, thanks to my mother, Ann Wiseman;

For everything else, thanks to Hannah.

CONTRIBUTORS

Rainer Warzecha is an outstanding German artist working with a wide range of materials, but concentrating on earth and natural materials since 1990; he welcomes collaborators in his 'eARThen enterprises.' He works outdoors, at sites throughout Europe, from May to October; in winter he is home in Berlin, Stuttgart or Bavaria concentrating on graphic, photographic, and writing projects. **www.interglotz.de**

Mark Lakeman is co-founder and Co-Director of Creative Vision for The City Repair Project, which engages people in the reclaiming of common culture and common places to express local vision, experience, and knowledge. Founded in 1996, City Repair serves and supports communities wherever it is called. Mark "undersees" the effort, and travels widely to help communities transform their own commons. **Cityrepair.org, 503-235-8946.**

Ed Raduazo worked at the US Patent & Trademark Office for 33 years, in building structures and plant husbandry. His second career is as a volunteer teacher. "One family fun class," says Ed, "raises $600 for Green Spring Gardens Park, and gives me a venue to talk about traditional societies and appropriate technology while we build bird houses using recycled materials and appropriate technology." **raduazo@aol.com**

Jamie Topper is a Chicago sculptor who learned natural building in Mexico and British Columbia, and has been using earthen materials and techniques to develop public art projects with children and communities. She says working with mud in the city helps her "begin to reconcile philosophies of sustainability with my city kitty 3rd floor apartment lifestyle." **773-782-3538, jtbaladi@yahoo.com.**

Kiko Denzer designs and builds walls, murals, installations, ovens, fireplaces, and other structures; he also teaches here and abroad, and occasionally exhibits sculpture in galleries. He started working with earth in 1994. Build Your Own Earth Oven, his popular manual on ovens, bread, and mud, has put thousands of hands in the dirt. He can be contacted through **Hand Print Press.**

RESOURCES

ART AND TEACHING:

Drawing with Children, by Mona Brookes, Jeremy Tarcher/Putnam, NYC, 1996. Breaks drawing down into a visual syntax and grammar; effective for teaching realistic drawing to all ages. A simple approach that also creates a positive, supportive environment for students and teacher.

Drawing on the Right Side of the Brain, by Betty Edwards, *Putnam.* Edwards teaches you to draw what your eye sees, rather than what your mind (thinks) it knows. Her techniques (e.g., drawing from an upside-down photo) are now standard teaching tools, Either new or old edition is recommended.

The Best of Making Things, A Handbook of Creative Discovery, by Ann Sayre Wiseman, Hand Print Press, 2005 (order form on page 127). 125 projects with clear, hand-drawn directions. A classic for learning by doing, originally developed for the Boston Children's Museum.

Hooked on Drawing: Illustrated Lessons & Exercises, by Sandy Brooke, Prentice Hall, NJ, 1996.

The Long Haul, by Miles Horton, with Judith & Herbert Kohl, Teachers College Press, 1998; Educational theory as stories, the central one of which is about the role of education in the civil rights movement. The essential lessons apply to any effort: any person can and will learn to help themselves, and we learn best when we feel "at home."

The Unknown Craftsman: A Japanes Insight into Beauty, by Soetsu Yanagi, Kodansha Intn'l, 1989; illustrated essays about craft, art, and aesthetics by one of Japan's most important thinkers; introduced by Bernard Leach. Addresses "the very nature of human life and work" and "the meaning of beauty in the face of truth."

EARTHEN BUILDING — TECHNICAL & HOW-TO:

Build Your Own Earth Oven, by Kiko Denzer, Hand Print Press, 2000, (see back of book to order). A good first project for building with earth.

The Cobber's Companion, by Michael Smith, Cob Cottage Company, Oregon, 2000. A simple, illustrated handbook for building an earthen home, by the folks who began the earth building revival in the US.

The Hand-Sculpted House, by Ianto Evans, Michael Smith, and Linda Smiley, Chelsea Green, White River Junction, Vermont, 2002. A more in-depth handbook for earthen building. LOTS of photos & illustrations.

The Art of Natural Building, Joseph F. Kennedy, Michael G. Smith and Catherine Wanek, editors; New Society Publishers, 2002, Canada.

Building with Earth, A Handbook, by John Norton, ITDG, 1997, London, itdgpublishing.org.uk.

The Natural Plaster Book: Earth, Lime and Gypsum Plasters for Natural Homes, by Cedar Rose Guelberth & Dan Chiras, New Society Publishers, 2003, Canada. Ms. Guelberth operates the Building for Health Materials Center, which supplies plastering tools and materials, including trowels, pigments, etc. POB 113, Carbondale CO 81623, 800-292-4838, buildingforhealth.com

A Pattern Language, Christopher Alexander, et al, Oxford U. Press; 1977. Explores patterns as the structures that make places *beautiful,* from town and transport patterns to details like windows, doors, and ornament.

The Nature of Order, (4 vols), Christopher Alexander, Center for Environmental Structure; 2002. Explains how beauty is an objective reality, rather than a subjective quality; connects scientific with intuitive knowledge. The first book includes a useful exploration of pattern, ornament, and their utility in building & architecture.

patternlanguage.com, Christopher Alexander et al, Center for Environmental Structure. Resources related to the above texts, and a source for the books (which every library should buy).

The Old Way of Seeing, by Jonathan Hale, Houghton Mifflin; 1994. More on the geometry of good buildings.

WORKSHOP PROVIDERS & OTHER PRACTITIONERS:

not an exhaustive list, but the following provide hands-on workshops for working with mud, and more. The field is growing, so a web search is worthwhile, especially on specific topics, like plastering and finishes.

Cob Cottage Company. POB 123, Cottage Grove, OR, 97424; 541-942-2005; cobcottage.com. Earthen and natural building; courses and internships; also coordinates permaculture and natural building workshops with Alejandra Caballero and Paco Gomez in Mexico.

Cobworks: c/o Pat Hennebery, RR#1 Mayne Island, BC, V0N2J0. cobworks.com (250)539-5253 pat or elke @cobworks.com. Hands-on workshops, presentations, teamwork, fun; internships.

The Canelo Project: Athena and Bill Steen were among the first to build with straw bale, and are expert plasterers who offer many worthwhile workshops and study tours; they are also the authors of *Built by Hand* (below). 520-455-5548; absteen@dakotacom.net; www.caneloproject.com.

Groundworks: Becky Bee; PO Box 381, Murphy, Oregon 97533 USA; 541-471-3470; www.beckybee.net; cobalot@cpros.com

City Repair, Portland, Oregon, working to make cities work for people. PO Box 42615 (1237 SE Stark) Portland, OR 97242 503-235-8946; thecircle@cityrepair.org cityrepair.org

EARTH-ARCHITECTURE & OTHER INSPIRATION:

African Painted Houses: Basotho Dwellings of Southern Africa, by Gary Van Wyk, Harry N. Abrams, NYC, 1998.

Butabu: Adobe Architecture of West Africa, Morris & Blier, Princeton Arch. Press, 2004.

Built by Hand: Vernacular Buildings around the World, Steen & Komatsu, Gibbs Smith, 2003.

Spectacular Vernacular: The Adobe Tradition, by Bourgeois and Pelos, Aperture, NYC, 1996.

African Canvas, Margaret C. Clarke, Rizzoli, 1990.

Architecture for the Poor, by Hassan Fathy, U. Chicago Press; 2000. A classic of "indigenous architecture."

Dirt, the Ecstatic Skin of the Earth, William Bryant Logan, Riverhead Books, 1995. Educational & provocative natural history.

SUNDIALS & MORE

Make a Simple Sundial, by Kiko Denzer, Hand Print Press, 2005; illustrated guide to dial-making, dial-geometry, and planetary relationships. (see order form).

Sun, Moon, & Earth, Robin Heath, 1999, Wooden Books, Walker & Co. Clear drawings and simple text explore and explain the logic of celestial movement; one of a wonderful series.

The Sun, Moon & Tides, AND Sundials and Timedials, by Gerald Jenkins & Magdalen Bear, 2000, Tarquin Publications. Working paper models and explanations.

Make a Sundial, British Sundial Society, 1993. Brief, easy, how-to.

Sundials, How to Know, Use, and Make them, By R. Newton Mayall, and Margaret L. Mayall, Boston, 1962, Charles T. Branford Co.

Sundials, Their Theory and Construction, Albert E. Waugh, 1973, Dover Publications.

Numbers, The Universal Language, by Denis Guedj, 1992, Harry N. Abrams.

Sacred Geometry, Philosophy and Practice, Robert Lawlor, 1982, Thames and Hudson.

Field Guide the to Night Sky, National Audobon Society, 1991, Chanticleer Press, Knopf.

Secrets of the Night Sky, Bob Berman, 1995, Harper Perennial.

Connecting with the Cosmos, Donald Goldsmith, 2002, Sourcebooks.

A Beginner's Guide to Constructing the Universe: The Mathematical Archetypes of Nature, Art, & Science: A Voyage from 1 to 10, Michael S. Schneider, 1994, Harper Collins. Essays and geometrical drawing exercises that illustrate the history and philosophy of ancient geometry and "earth-measure."

Stone Circles: A Modern Builder's Guide to the Megalithic Revival, Rob Roy, 1999, Chelsea Green. A natural builder's guide to stone circles, ancient & modern.

HAND PRINT PRESS
"WHAT WE LEARN TO DO, WE LEARN BY DOING" — ARISTOTLE

THE BEST OF MAKING THINGS, A HANDBOOK OF CREATIVE DISCOVERY, BY ANN SAYRE WISEMAN

125 projects carefully selected by the author to "develop natural curiosity and self-esteem," and to demonstrate "simple and important concepts that have shaped the cultures of the world." So when a child asks, "what can I do," you can say: "Make paper from laundry lint! A bird feeder from clothes hangers! Chocolate pudding finger paintings! Fish & potato prints! A cardboard box loom to weave on! Simple shirts, pants or dresses!" The author's detailed and delightful drawings fill every page: "so that children just starting out and grown-ups who have missed out can quickly grasp the ideas." 178 illustrated pages, 6x9 inch budget edition is child-sized, indexed. $8.95.

BUILD YOUR OWN EARTH OVEN, A LOW-COST, WOOD-FIRED MUD OVEN, SIMPLE SOURDOUGH BREAD, PERFECT LOAVES, BY KIKO DENZER

A practical intro to earthen building and wood-fired ovens. If you can make mud pies, you can make an oven. And bake really good bread! Simple, straightforward, inspiring, & fully illustrated! 5 stars on Amazon. "Creative. Innovative. Brilliant. ...the definitive book on how to build an adobe oven. – www.williamrubel.com. "Brief, brisk, artful, and well-written....empowering throughout." – Permaculture Activist. 134 pages, color photos, indexed, 7x10 inches, $14.95.

MAKE A SIMPLE SUNDIAL: MEASURE THE EARTH, DISCOVER THE COSMOS, BY KIKO DENZER

How to make an accurate sundial with simple materials: locate true north; feel the earth turn underfoot; understand time and the the axis it turns on. See how your dial models the relationship between the earth and the sun – and between you and the cosmos.. 32 pages, 4-1/4x7 inches, illustrated, $4.95.

DIG YOUR HANDS IN THE DIRT, A MANUAL FOR MAKING ART OUT OF EARTH, BY KIKO DENZER

Inspiration and instruction for making beautiful and practical art with the most basic (and cheap) material. LOTS of photos of projects done by mudfolks near & far. 128 pages, 32 in color, 5x8-1/2. $12.95.

EARTH ART, A CATALOG, BY KIKO DENZER

Unusual & beautiful natural shapes and patterns in earthen plaster; 24 pages of full color photos with text, 8-1/2 × 11 inches, $20.

QUICK ORDER FORM

PLEASE SEND THE FOLLOWING BOOKS:

TITLE .... QUANTITY

_____

_____

_____

_____

_____

_____

_____

SHIP TO (PLEASE INCLUDE PHONE/EMAIL):

_____

_____

_____

_____

SHIPPING

US: $3 for the first book, $2 each additional (media mail)
CANADA: $5 for the first book, $3 each additional (air mail)
INTERNATIONAL: $10 the first book, $3 ea. addt'l (air mail)
Send check or money order, in US CURRENCY ONLY to:
POB 576, Blodgett OR 97326
For more info: www.handprintpress.com
541-438-4300

BOOK TRADE:

Our distributor to the book trade, except for the Sundial book
and Earth Art catalog, is Chelsea Green, www.cheseagreen.com,
1-800-639-4099.

For my mother, who gave me my hands

At work in Tlaxco, Mexico, 1996

An artist
is not a special kind of person;
every person
is a special kind of artist.
— Eric Gill